ROCK
'TIL
YOU
DROP

by Steve Butterworth

ROCK 'TIL YOU DROP
by Steve Butterworth

Published by Eye 5 - 2004
ISBN: 0-9546897-2-0

Eye 5
www.eye5.org.uk
15 Spruce Avenue
Great Dunmow
Essex CM6 1YY
United Kingdom

Design by Eye 5

CONTENTS

ROCK 'TIL YOU DROP

Musicians who failed to reach 40

INTRODUCTION

Some people are just asking for it. Others have no choice. The music world is littered with young casualties. Some died by misadventure, some intentionally by their own hand, some tragically.

People in hazardous occupations tend to have more chance of reaching a ripe old age than your average rocker. You don't have to be a Cobain, a Hendrix or a gangsta rapper to warrant an early grave. The fickle finger of fate has shown no favouritism in calling time before time is statistically up.

Why do musicians die younger than in other professions?

It may be the lifestyle - an incessant diet of sex and drugs and rock 'n roll can be damaging to your health.

It may be their art is the key; the pain of creation. The urge to create is the urge to destroy, to mangle the anarchists' favourite slogan.

Of course, rock victims never set out to destroy themselves. Most just want to make music. Wallowing in the riches and excesses of their world comes hand-in-hand to some, and is a natural progression, wittingly or unwittingly, for others.

'Dead', for instance. So his real name was a mouthful to the English-speaking world, but calling himself 'Dead' and singing for a death metal band called 'Mayhem' seems to be inviting a sordid end.

'Dead' blew his brains out.

Rock stars don't require morbid pseudonyms, though, to ask for it.

Even the boy/girl-next-door types can degenerate into the rock subculture and prepare to meet their maker in a drink or drug-fuelled haze. Or in a plane crash, a hospital bed, a back alley, a dingy hotel room - or even onstage.

Plane travel is, in fact, safe - really safe.

The terrorist attacks in 2001 persuaded many Americans to stay at home. Were they aware that driving is TWENTY times riskier in the States?

Musicians have a poor track record with air travel, however. Some of the giants of the 20th century recording scene crashed to their deaths from the heavens.

The road cost many more their lives, literally.

Road accidents are the biggest cause of death by accident worldwide. You have a much greater chance of dying in a car than in war or a fire or at sea. The young are particularly prone; and men three times more at risk than women.

Young males, notably Americans, are also likely to be victims of murderers - or, indeed, murderers themselves.

Europeans are more likely to kill themselves - suicide being responsible for twice as many deaths.

Guns and drugs are the preferred choice of exit.

Disease strikes anyone, anywhere. Heart ailments and cancer top the league table.

The musicians on these pages - the legends and the footnotes of the modern era - have one thing in common: they all died before reaching 40, that milestone year when Joe Average hits the middle-aged blues and starts the countdown to retirement.

Somewhere their memories linger on.

Steve Butterworth – October 2004

MURDER

CRAZIES, criminals, jealous colleagues, jilted lovers and even terrorists - rarely a day goes by without the news bringing forth tales of madness and murder.

Considering their lifestyles, it may be surprising that not more rock stars have been murder victims; or that more have not been compelled to commit murder. The bigger the star name, the greater the number of heavies engaged to protect them – primarily from overly-obsessive fans in the wake of John Lennon's fatal shooting in 1980 (the former Beatle was 40 and outside our remit).

But security is a modern trend. When Robert Johnson was plying his trade down in the delta, you looked after yourself as best as you could. If you cared.

Robert Leroy Johnson, the King Of The Delta blues, died from drinking poisoned whisky on August 16th 1938. He was 27.

In the summer of 1938 he was playing at Greenwood, Mississippi, and became a little too-friendly with the wife of the Three Forks store/club owner. During an interval on the Saturday night Johnson was hanging out with Sonny Boy Williamson when he was handed a bottle of whisky laced with strychnine.

He was unable to complete his set. He lingered for several weeks in a private home before dying on August 16th. Johnson was buried in a simple wooden coffin provided by the authorities. His final resting place remains a source of speculation.

The Mt. Zion Missionary Baptist Church near Morgan City, Mississippi maintains the Robert Johnson Memorial, which was donated by Columbia Records. According to Johnson's death certificate, he's buried in the Mt. Zion graveyard.

But David 'Honeyboy' Edwards, who was with Johnson when he died, said Johnson's sister moved his remains to Payne Chapel Missionary Baptist

Church in nearby Quito. Did Johnson really sell his soul to the devil? Only he, the Lord and Lucifer know whether or not his talent was God-given or the result of a satanic pact. No-one at the time could play like him. Contemporaries claimed he could hear a song just once and then perform it himself note-perfect.

He studied at the feet of some Blues legends: Charlie Patton, Son House, Sonny Boy Williamson, Elmore James, Howlin' Wolf and Memphis Slim.

Johnson married twice. His first wife was just 16 when she and the baby she was carrying died in childbirth. He deserted his second wife and took to travelling the deep south, writing songs and performing anywhere that would allow. He developed a taste for booze and gambling. He'd had an eye for the ladies since his youth. His extra-curricula activities proved his downfall. The Rolling Stones headed a line of post-60s groups who helped rekindle interest in Johnson's music.

Blues legend **Sonny Boy Williamson** (born John Lee Williamson) died after suffering multiple injuries (including a fractured skull) during mugging after leaving a Chicago club on June 1st 1948. He was 34.

"In his mouth and hands, the harmonica learned to wail and chirp, laugh and cry, in spanking new rhythms and to daring new beats," reads Williamson's gravestone in Jackson, Tennessee. The Tennessee State Historic Commission arranged for the new stone to replace the decaying old metal marker 42 years after his death.

Lousiana-born **Little Walter**, like Williamson a renowned harp player, died on February 15th 1968 following a street fight during which he was beaten with an iron bar.

Walter was a womaniser, gambler and heavy drinker - it is uncertain which of his vices sparked the brawl.

A woman proved fatal for **Stacy Sutherland**, guitar player with The 13th Floor Elevators, a 1960s psychedelic band from Austin, Texas.

He was killed by his wife on August 24th 1978. He was 32.

The band sang about drugs, and drugs proved its demise. Sutherland served time for drug offences and was battling heroin addiction.

His estranged wife, Bunny Unger, shot him in the stomach in a domestic dispute at her house. No charges were filed.

Soul singer/songwriter **Sam Cooke** was shot dead in a motel on December 11th 1964. He was 33.

Cooke, raised in a preacher's family in Chicago, recorded massive hits such as Twistin' the Night Away, You Send Me, Only Sixteen and Havin' A Party which were covered by many artists over the years.

On the eve of his death, Cooke had met a 22-year-old woman, Elisa Boyer, at a bar in Los Angeles. They went to a Sunset Boulevard nightclub before checking into the Hacienda Motel in the early hours of December 11th. What happened next is open to speculation even four decades later. A scantily-clad Boyer fled the room carrying most of Cooke's clothes and her own. Unable to raise anyone at the office, she went to phone the police from a payphone.

Manageress Bertha Franklin answered the door when Cooke went looking for Boyer. She told him she didn't know where the girl was. Cooke returned a few minutes later, broke into the manager's office and, during a struggle, was shot three times by Franklin.

Franklin told authorities Cooke was in a violent mood, had tried to rape Boyer and that she shot him out of fear for herself.

The coroner pronounced a verdict of justifiable homicide. One month after Cooke's death, Boyer was arrested in Hollywood for prostitution.

Cooke was inducted into the Rock And Roll Hall of Fame in 1986.

Philadelphia-born trumpet player **Lee Morgan** was shot dead on February 19th 1972 at Slug's Club in New York. He was 33.

Morgan, who had performed with Dizzy Gillespie's band, was playing with his quintet when his current girlfriend Helen More shot him. He died on stage.

Carlton Barrett, drummer with reggae giants The Wailers, was shot dead outside his Kingston, Jamaica home on April 17th 1987. He was 36.

His wife, Albertine, her lover, Glenroy Carter, and Junior Neil were charged with his killing. Albertine and Carter escaped the rap, and were sentenced to seven years for conspiracy. Carlton (aka Field Marshal) with his younger brother Aston on bass, acted as the backbone of the unique Bob Marley and The Wailers sound.

Musical rivals can be just as vicious as lovers. **Oystein Aarseth**, guitarist and leader with Norwegian death metal band Mayhem, was stabbed to death by a colleague outside his Oslo flat on August 10th 1993. He was 26.

Varg Vikernes (aka Count Grishnackh) was sentenced to 21 years jail for the brutal slaying. It was the culmination of a power battle between the pair. Some claim Vikernes murdered Aarseth (aka Euronymous) because of his alleged homosexuality. Others say they were at odds over the direction of the Norwegian black metal (or death metal) scene. Were they followers of satan or merely against Christianity and seeking a return to Norway's ancient pagan traditions? Then again, it may have been a dispute over money and Count Grisnackh's wages.

Whatever the reason, he arrived at Aarseth's flat in a foul mood and chased the barely-clad band leader down four flights of stairs, inflicting 25 stab wounds. Aarseth owned a record store called Helvete (hell) and was guitarist and founder of Mayhem; Vikernes stepped in on bass after two members had quit - he was also leader of Burzum, his own one-man band.

At his trial Vikernes was also convicted of arson attacks on three churches and the death of a fireman who tackled one of his blazes. The pagan traditionalists were heavily into arson.

Vikernes escaped in October 2003 when given temporary leave from his low-security prison. He was expected to be released in two years. He was quickly captured after forcing a family at gunpoint to hand over their Volvo.

He had written to his mother revealing his intentions to break jail after a fellow inmate had tried to strangle him.

Aarseth was reunited with former bandmate **'Dead'** (born **Per Yngve Ohlin**) in the underworld. Aarseth had feasted on Dead's brain after finding his corpse on April 8th 1991. Dead was dead at 20, having shot himself in the head.

The Mayhem singer's suicide note read: "Excuse all the blood." Aarseth found the body, and took photos for a future album cover and consumed fragments of his brain matter after mixing it with stew. Drummer Hellhammer made a necklace using some of his skull fragments.

American jazz band leader **James Reese Europe** was stabbed to death by his drummer on May 19th 1919. He was 38.

During an interval at a show in Boston, Herbert Wright, one of twins who played percussion in the band, attacked Europe with a penknife. He was angry at what he considered favouritism shown to his brother.

The wound appeared minor, requiring a few stitches. But the knife had sliced Europe's jugular vein and he died from loss of blood.

Bobby Ramirez, drummer with several bands including Edgar Winter's White Trash, was beaten in a Chicago brawl on July 24th 1972 because of his long hair. He was 23.

Singer Jerry LaCroix's reply to a question on The Ultimate Edgar Winter Fansite (www.winternet.us) detailed Ramirez's end:

I will try and shed some light on the terrible event we had in Chicago that led to the death of one of my dearest and closest friends, Bobby Ramirez...we were on tour with Uriah Heep playing all the big halls(10,000 seaters) to sold out crowds.

Uriah Heep and my band LaCroix got along swimmingly, as the English say. We really enjoyed each other's company and got along great on and off stage. I had just released my first solo album and the tour was going along wonderfully. The contrasting styles of the two bands just seemed to work magic on the crowds. We had finished a great night (Rosemont Hall?) and were out on the town for some fun and relaxation. Rush Street was where the action was.

We found a club where an all-girl band, Bertha – some friends of ours from LA –

were playing and went in and found a spot in the balcony. The girls were really hot...they were rockin'. The little drummer played with such dynamics.

We were yelling and encouraging them on, just having the time of our lives. The show was over. Bobby went downstairs to take a leak. Our road manager came back upstairs and anxiously reported that Bobby had had an altercation in the bathroom.

I ran downstairs to find out what was happening. Bobby told me that while he was standing over the urinal the guy next to him made a comment about his long hair. Mind you we are in the longhair part of town in Chicago!

Evidently, Bobby said something back to the guy who, by the way, was also of Mexican descent, who then struck a blow to Bobby's cheek which drew blood.

By the time I got downstairs everyone was standing in the middle of the dance floor. Bobby, the club manager, the guy that hit him and onlookers.

Bobby wanted to report the incident to the police. The manager was just trying to get us to go home and so was I, but I could see Bobby's point. This guy obviously didn't belong down here with all the rest of us. He was dressed in slacks with sharp pointed shoes and his hair was short and slicked back.

I believe that he was there to do just what he did. I tried to coax Bobby out and let's just "blow it off" - one of his favorite expressions - but he couldn't believe that someone could assault him (or anyone else) in a public place and get away with it!

He went out the front door by himself. I followed. He was at the corner leaning against the lamp post with his head down and I shouted 'come on Bobby let's go', but he went around the corner and down the block.

When I got to the corner I saw him half-way down the street when someone came running out of the alley and attacked. I ran to his assistance when another person came out of the alley and grabbed me by the hair and said 'oh you want some, too' and commenced kicking me repeatedly between the eyes with pointed shoes.

I was of absolutely no help. I'd never been in a fight in my life. I went down. When I recovered a little they were gone and our road manager was there on his knees with Bobby's bloody head in his arms. This has been extremely difficult for me to report but it's time the world should know what really happened that dreadful night. There's hardly a day goes by when I don't think about dear Bobby and what 1,000 things I could have done differently.

A beating at a club also ended the tragic life of **John 'Jaco' Pastorius**, bass player with Weather Report. Pastorius died on September 21st 1987. He was 35. He had lain in a coma for nine days after being beaten sense-less by a bouncer at a Florida club.

Born in Pennsylvania, Jaco made his name in the New York jazz scene. Sadly, he developed depression and sought treatment (voluntary and later at the insistence of the authorities).

By the mid-80s the self-styled World's Greatest Bass Player was out of control, deserted by fed-up musician colleagues, drinking heavily, taking cocaine and hanging out at the wrong places in Florida. He would beg for bread and sleep wherever he could lay his head, usually on the street or in a park. He was arrested many times for minor offences. In a desperate attempt to display his undoubted musical prowess he would crash gigs and try to join in with whichever band was on stage.

The night before he was battered he jumped onstage during a Santana concert in Fort Lauderdale. Then on September 12th he tried to crash the Midnight Club in Lauderdale – a late-night joint. The 25-year-old nightclub bouncer did not know who the World's Greatest Bass Player was and the fatal fight ensued.

Bobby Fuller was found dead in his mother's Oldsmobile in Los Angeles on July 18th 1966. He was 23.

He had returned home from a stressful tour, and the coroner recorded a verdict of suicide - yet most believe Fuller was murdered.

His body showed signs of a beating, was covered in gasoline and there was gasoline in his lungs. American TV programme "Unsolved Mysteries" investigated several theories.

Earlier in the year, his band The Bobby Fuller Four had celebrated their biggest hit single - I Fought The Law, composed by Sonny Curtis who had been a guitarist with Buddy Holly's Crickets.

Phil King, one-time singer with metal band Blue Oyster Cult, was killed during a fight in New York on April 27th 1972. He was 27. King was shot dead during a quarrel with a gambling associate who owed him money.

Rhett Forrester, vocalist with New York metal band Riot, was shot dead in his car in Atlanta on January 22nd 1994. He was 37.

Atlanta police reported that two men approached Forrester while he was stopped at an intersection. A witness said he overheard arguing then one of the men shot Forrester in the back. The bullet pierced his heart, yet Forrester was able to drive a few blocks where he flagged down a police car. The only words he spoke to the officer were "I've been shot!" He then collapsed and died.

Friends established a fund to help police bring to justice their chief suspect. Police claim lack of concrete evidence has delayed any arrest.

Police did eventually press charges in the murder of **Mia Zapata** – ten years after her death. Zapata, lead singer with Seattle punk band The Gits, was strangled with the cord of her sweatshirt on July 7th 1993. She was 27.

Her body was found by a roadside two hours after she had left a Seattle bar, the Comet Tavern on Capitol Hill. She was lying in a cross shape – with her arms outstretched and her ankles crossed – leading some to believe the murder was ritualistic. Despite heavy Press and TV coverage, it was not until almost ten years later that a 48-year-old Cuban fisherman, Jesus Mezquia was charged with her murder.

Police got their break when a DNA check through the national criminal database revealed a match. DNA technology had advanced and in June 2002 police were able to extract DNA from a cotton swab containing saliva from the murderer.

Florida authorities put the DNA profile from Mezquia into the national database in November. The Seattle department dealing with unsolved crimes had their match.

Mezquia has an extensive criminal history in Florida and in California. Convictions include battery of a pregnant woman in 1997 and possessing burglary tools in 2002. He also was arrested for soliciting, kidnapping, false imprisonment and indecent exposure.

In Palm Springs, California he was convicted of battery and assault and battery of a spouse and was arrested for rape, robbery and indecent exposure. Charging papers also reveal that five weeks after the Zapata murder, a woman reported a car following her in the area near the murder scene. She said the man exposed himself. She got the license plate number. The car was registered to Jesus Mezquia.

He was arrested in January 2003 and after several hearings was convicted of Zapata's murder in March 2004, and a few weeks later sentenced to 36 years.

Saxophonist **King Curtis** (born Curtis Ousley) was stabbed to death outside his New York appartment on August 13th 1971. He was 37.

One of his most famous solos was on the Coasters' hit Yakety Yak. He played with a host of artists, including The Beatles, Eric Clapton, Buddy Holly, The Drifters and Aretha Franklin.

He had recently finished working with John Lennon on the Imagine album when he was killed. Curtis was carrying an air conditioner into his appartment on West 86th Street. Two junkies started abusing him, and one of them, Juan Montañez, knifed him in the heart.

He was rushed to Roosevelt Hospital, but pronounced dead on arrival. Rev. Jesse Jackson preached at his funeral – Aretha Franklin and others sang. Atlantic Records closed their office for the day in his honour.

Detroit rocker **Rusty Day**, singer with heavy metal bands Cactus and The Amboy Dukes, was murdered on June 3rd, 1982 in Orlando. He was 26.

Born Russell Edward Davidson, he enjoyed his greatest success with Cactus whose three albums earned them a long-lasting hardcore fan base.

Guitarist Ted Nugent, who went on to greater things, told an interviewer: "I was involved with firing him (from Amboys) because he insisted on doing LSD together as a band.

"After I fired him he was machine-gunned to death because of a bad drug deal. Rusty, his son, and a neighbour's boy were all killed...all killed in Orlando. Damn shame."

Arlester Christian (aka Dyke), singer and bass guitarist with Dyke & The Blazers, was shot dead by a lunatic in Phoenix, Arizona, on March 13th 1971. He was 27.

The Blazers had made Phoenix their base in the mid-60s after being stranded there by The O'Jays. They were backing The O'Jays who couldn't afford the fares to take the boys back to Buffalo, New York.

Dyke and The Blazers went it alone and made one massive hit in 1966 – Funky Broadway, written by Dyke to accompany a dance he had invented.

Texan singer/song-writer **Blaze Foley** was shot dead in Austin on February 1st 1989. He was 39.

Foley (born Michael David Fuller) died in hospital after being shot by Carey January. Foley was trying to protect January's father, Concho, when he was killed with a .22 rifle. There had been acrimony between the pair in the past. Carey January was acquitted by the jury, who believed his evidence that he acted in self-defence.

Foley performed with his mother, brother and sisters in the Fuller Family, a gospel group, before going solo.

A news agency reported the following shortly after his death:

Singer-songwriter Townes Van Zandt, who knew Foley for about 10 years, said that aside from his songs, Foley would be remembered for his "generosity down to his last penny," his wit - and his duct tape.

He was unsure how Foley grew attached to duct tape, but said it became his trademark. "He'd get a new pair of shoes and put duct tape (on them) to dress them up," Van Zandt said. "He was a friend of the homeless, poor, elderly, a real super caring guy. And he would sometimes seem bitter, you know. The only reason for that is he was brimming over with so much genuine love and caring.

"To see an injustice sometimes it would just put him over to a frenzy, kind of. He couldn't stand to see a poor bag lady on the street. It threw him into a rage, almost. It just came from love."

Foley was buried with duct tape adorning his coffin.

James Sheppard, singer with doo-wop band Shep & the Limelights, was robbed and beaten to death in his car in New York on January 24th 1970. He was 33.

Al Jackson, drummer with Booker T. and the MGs, was shot dead by a burglar at his Memphis home on October 1st 1975. He was 39. Booker T. Jones and his band launched the 'Memphis Sound' and were the amazing backers at Stax-Volt for stars such as Otis Redding, Sam & Dave and many more. Jackson produced blues guitarist Albert King.

Plans for the MGs to reform were under way when Jackson was killed.

Texas-born singer **Selena** (born Selena Quintanilla-Perez) was shot dead by her fan club president on March 31st 1995. She was 24.

Selena, who had recently wed her guitarist Chris Perez, was killed by Yolanda Saldivar during a meeting at a Days Inn motel in Corpus Christi, Texas. Selena had accused Saldivar of stealing funds from the business accounts. Saldivar, a former nurse, was sentenced to life by a Houston court the following year.

After receiving death threats, she was placed in an isolation block and chained to guards for her one-hour-a-day exercise time.

Saldivar insisted she never stole from her 'daughter' and that the shooting was an accident, claiming she pointed a gun at her own head during the argument. She said she was motioning toward Selena and telling her not to close the door when the gun went off.

Paul Avron Jeffreys, bass player with British band Cockney Rebel, and his wife Rachel were killed in the terrorist attack on Pan Am Flight 103 over Lockerbie on December 21st 1988. Paul was 36, Rachel 23. They were heading to New York for their honeymoon.

Thirty-eight minutes after taking off from London, the Boeing 747 exploded over the Scottish town of Lockerbie, killing all 259 onboard. Eleven people were killed as debris rained down on Lockerbie.

Semtex, a virtually undetectable explosive, was placed in a suitcase by terrorists acting with Libyan connivance.

Two Libyan intelligence agents, Abdel Basset Ali al-Megrahi and Lamen Khalifa Fhimah, were named as suspects and charged after many years of international wrangling.

Al-Megrahi was found guilty in January 2001 at a special court in the Netherlands and sentenced to life. Fhimah was acquitted.

Cockney Rebel had a smash-hit with Make Me Smile (Come Up And See Me) in 1975.

Michael Menson died in Billericay Hospital, Essex, on February 13th 1997 – 16 days after being torched by a gang of racists in London. He was 30.

Michael Tachie-Menson, who enjoyed several UK hits in the 80s with reggae group Double Trouble, was found on fire on the North Circular Road, Edmonton. Police believed he had tried to commit suicide. They didn't treat the incident as murder until Menson told his brother he had been attacked.

They had tried to set fire to Menson's coat with a lighter. When that proved unsuccessful they returned and doused him in white spirit, stole his personal stereo and set him on fire.

Motorists found him still aflame on the road.

At the trial in December 1999, student Mario Pereira was convicted of murder and Barry Charalambous Constantinou, of manslaughter. Both men and Husseyin Abdullah were also found guilty of perverting justice.

Shirley Brickley, singer with Philadelphia R&B group The Orlons, was shot dead in her hometown on October 13th 1977. She was 32. The Orlons enjoyed a Number Two USA hit with The Wah Wahtsui in 1961.

Rap and violence go hand in hand.

Scott La Rock (born Scott Sterling) was one of the first to suffer a violent death. He was shot dead while trying to break up an argument at a party in the Bronx, New York, on August 25th 1987.

Mr C (Hubert 'Kyle' Church III), of San Francisco rappers RBL Posse, was gunned down while chatting with friends on a street on New Year's Eve 1995. On February 4th 2003 RBL's **Hitman** was shot and killed while driving his car.

Randy 'Stretch' Walker, a member of the rap group Live Squad, was shot dead in Queens, New York, on November 30th 1995. Police quizzed a suspect concerning the Stretch killing and that of Jam Master Jay.

Jam Master Jay, however, came before the mould was made and seemed outside the savage world inhabited by the gangsta rappers. JMJ was was shot dead on October 30th 2002. He was 37. Born Jason Mizell, the DJ/turntable-scratcher with Run-DMC, was gunned down early in the evening at a recording studio in Queens, New York. A 25-year-old man was hospitalised after being shot in the ankle.

Witnesses described the shooter as a young black man in a white sweatsuit or sweatshirt, according to news reports.

Police said two gunmen were buzzed into the building, went up to the second-floor studio and shot Jam Master Jay once at close range.

Run-DMC united rap 'n rock in their 1986 remake of Aerosmith's Walk This Way. Eighteen months after the shooting, no arrests had been made.

Violence, gangs and brushes with the law were part of **Tupac Shakur's** regular existence. He died on September 13th 1996 – six days after being shot in Las Vegas. He was 25.

Shakur's five-car motorcade was heading for a nightclub after watching the Mike Tyson-Bruce Seldon fight at the MGM Grand Hotel. Marion 'Suge' Knight, head of Death Row Records, and Shakur were in Knight's black BMW 750 when a man opened fire from a white Cadillac.

Knight suffered a minor bullet graze but Shakur was critically wounded. The Los Angeles Times reported:

The attack was the latest and most lethal episode in the checkered lives of the two men. Shakur has been arrested at least half a dozen times in the past three years.

Knight has boasted publicly that at least three contracts are out on his life.

At a 1992 outdoor festival in Marin County, Shakur was involved in a scuffle that left a six-year-old child dead from a stray bullet. The following year, he was accused – but never convicted – of shooting two off-duty Atlanta police officers and then of attacking a fellow rapper with a baseball bat at a concert in Michigan.

Then, while on trial for sexual assault in November 1994, Shakur was shot five times during a robbery in the lobby of a New York recording studio.

The performer, who lost $40,000 worth of jewelry in the incident, was later convicted on the sexual assault charges and served eight months in a New York penitentiary before being released last year pending appeal.

Knight has been criticised for promoting violence and explicit sex in gangsta rap. And he was charged with assault with a deadly weapon – but not convicted – for allegedly pulling a gun on two aspiring rappers in 1992 after a dispute over the use of an office telephone.

Shakur's group had been to Knight's Vegas home after the Tyson fight and were driving to Club 662 (owned by Knight) when the shooting occurred.

Eye-witnesses said four men were in the white Cadillac.

The convoy continued to drive erratically for several blocks before the vehicles came to a stop across from the Aladdin Hotel. Shakur was taken to the University Medical Center.

Fans prayed and held a vigil outside the hospital. "I'm a strong believer in God," his mother said. "And I know he'll make it."

Shakur died on September 13th.

New York rapper Notorious B.I.G., soon to follow Shakur to an early grave, was later alleged to have been behind Shakur's death.

Notorious B.I.G. (aka Biggie Smalls) was shot dead in Los Angeles on March 9th 1997. He was 24. Born Christopher G. L. Wallace, Notorious B.I.G. was returning from a party when he was gunned down in his car. He died soon after reaching a nearby hospital.

Thousands of rap fans flocked to his funeral in his native Brooklyn. Chaos ensued and police were forced to arrest unruly mourners. Fellow rappers released 'I'll be Missing You' in tribute. Proceeds from the million-seller went to his children.

Notorious B.I.G. Day followed on May 14th when hundreds of American radio stations aired 30 seconds of silence after spinning the single.

His murder was classed as a gangland slaying, possibly revenge for his involvement in the killing of rival rapper Shakur.

Biggie left a star-studded Vibe magazine party after the Soul Train Music Awards. When his green Chevy Suburban stopped at traffic lights, a dark Chevy Impala pulled up alongside. The driver, a black male in a suit and bow tie, rolled down his window and fired seven shots from a blue steel

9mm semi-automatic into the front passenger door. Four of the bullets hit Biggie, who died shortly after he arrived at Cedars-Sinai Medical Center.

Three years later, former LAPD detective Russell Poole claimed police corruption hindered his investigation into the B.I.G. murder. His investigations had revealed the involvement of a bent cop, David Mack, who was serving time for a bank robbery. Mack had links with LA gangs, rappers and drug dealers.

He owned a black Chevy Impala.

He was identified by one of Biggie's associates.

He had a shrine to Shakur in his home.

Poole quit the force in frustration, and the murder of Biggie remains unsolved.

The Los Angeles Times delivered a bombshell in 2002, claiming Biggie had offered gang members $1m to kill rival rapper Tupac Shakur and provided the gun used in his 1996 murder.

Reporter Chuck Philips claimed Biggie was in Las Vegas on the night of the shooting and met members of the Los Angeles Crips mob and gave them a loaded .40-calibre Glock pistol.

Orlando Anderson, a Crips gang member, was the shooter, according to Phillips. Shakur and members of his entourage had beaten up Anderson earlier that evening after the Mike Tyson-Bruce Seldon fight at the MGM Grand Hotel. The Crips wanted revenge - and the fact that Biggie was paying was a bonus.

Two years after Tupac's death, Anderson was shot dead in a car wash during a row over money.

New York rapper **Big L** (Lamont Coleman) was shot dead near his home in Harlem, New York, on February 15th 1999. He was 24.

He had been shot nine times, apparently in connection with a feud between his brother, who was in jail, and a local drug dealer.

Seattle rapper **Priceless Game** was shot dead on August 13th 2002. He was 23. Priceless Game (born Phillip Tyrone Griffin) was in the process of finishing his first album when he encountered some men in Seattle's International District. He was shot, tried to escape but collapsed and died in a car park.

Tony Pharr, who had served time in jail with P.G., was arrested later in the year. P.G. had a string of offences to his name: assault, robbery, theft and weapons charges.

Brazilian rapper **Sabotage** (Mauro Mateus dos Santos) was shot dead in Sao Paulo on January 24th 2003 while returning from a party. He was 29.

Santos, a well-known local drug dealer before his music career took off, was hit four times in the head and chest.

Camoflauge (born Jason Johnson) was shot dead in front of his 16-month-old son in Savannah, Georgia, on May 19th 2003. He was 21.

They were outside the office of his label, Pure Pain Records, when he was murdered. Police believe it was a revenge hit.

Cocaine dealer Felix Scott had been murdered a few days earlier and it is believed his associates were acting on a list of names he left behind.

Camoflauge and two other men had been killed in a spate of shootings which shocked the city.

Rapper **Soulja Slim** (born James Tapp) was shot dead on the lawn of his mother's home in New Orleans on November 26th 2003. He was 25.

Slim, who had served time for armed robbery, specialised in violent, drug-laced lyrics. Shortly before his death he had been involved in scuffles at several clubs, and there were reports of a $300,000 contract on his head.

A 22-year-old man was arrested on December 31st 2003.

ACCIDENT

THE AUTHOR was celebrating his second birthday on the day the music died – February 3rd 1959. It would be several years - and much music under the bridge – before I realised the music had died.

The music died, we are informed, in a plane wreckage. Fate had been cruel once again, robbing the world of three young talents.

Fate has a long history of such cruelty.

Sixty thousand perished in the great Lisbon earthquake of 1755. An angry God was punishing the city's sinners and the innocents got embroiled in the conflict. God is not on record as revealing why he chose Lisbon from a selection of 18th century Sin Cities. Nor why Buddy Holly's plane crashed en route to a gig; nor why Marc Bolan's car ploughed into a tree; nor why Harry Chapin's fuel tank caught fire.

Chapin was a long-standing charity worker and on his way to a benefit concert that fateful day – an innocent dying to warn the sinners?

According to Mark Twain: "There ain't no such thing as an accident; there ain't nothing happens in the world but what's ordered just so by a wiser power than us, and it's always for a good purpose ... whenever a thing happens that you think is an accident you make up your mind it ain't no accident at all - it's a special providence."

So special providence claimed the lives of rock 'n rollers **Buddy Holly** (22), The **Big Bopper** (24) and **Richie Valens** (17) that February 3rd.

Holly chartered a plane to fly to Fargo, North Dakota after a show in Clear Lake, Iowa. The Big Bopper (aka J.P. Richardson) and Richie Valens, who were touring with Holly, were onboard after asking band members Waylon Jennings and Tommy Allsup to give up their seats on the plane and take the tour bus instead.

Flight control became alarmed soon after take-off as pilot Roger Peterson had not contacted them by radio. The plane was discovered in a field the following day - all four travellers were dead. Twelve years later, their deaths would be labelled 'the day the music died' in Don McLean's hit single American Pie. Buddy Holly's fame is immense considering his death at such an early age.

He was born Charles Hardin Holley in Lubbock, Texas, and started performing at local clubs as soon as he hit his teens.

Buddy Holly and The Crickets supported Elvis and Bill Haley early in their career and were signed up by Decca records (the label's UK arm would later turn down The Beatles). They were one of the first major groups to write their own material. Catchy tunes flowed: Oh Boy!, Not Fade Away, That'll Be The Day, Peggy Sue.

A tour to Britain brought them much claim and fame abroad in 1958. That year Holly met Maria Elena Santiago, proposed on their first date and married a fortnight later.

The Crickets soon split up over musical differences and Buddy was touring with a new band when he took that fateful plane ride. Maria suffered a miscarriage after hearing of her husband's death. Holly was inducted into the Rock And Roll Hall Of Fame when it was launched in January 1986.

The Big Bopper (born Jiles Perry Richardson in Sabine Pass, Texas) was initially a DJ and once broadcasted continuously for FIVE days.

As The Big Bopper, his biggest hit was Chantilly Lace though he did write and sing backing vocals on Running Bear for Johnny Preston. The single became a Number One hit ten months after Bopper's death.

Richie Valens (born Richard Steven Valenzuela in Los Angeles) was on the tour to promote his double A-side single Donna/La Bamba.

David Box was one of the vocalists to play with The Crickets after Holly's death. He sang lead on the hit Peggy Sue Got Married. Like Holly, he died in a plane crash – on October 23rd 1964. He was 21.

Harold David Box was with a Houston band, Buddy and the Kings. Drummer Bill Daniels, a qualified pilot, hired a plane to take them to a gig in Harris County, Texas. Box, Daniels, singer Buddy Groves and bass player Carl Banks died when the plane crashed on the return flight.

Grand Ole Opry star **Patsy Cline** was killed in a plane crash on March 5th 1963. She was 30. Cline (born Virginia Patterson Hensley) and her band were returning to Nashville from a benefit concert in Kansas City for the family of DJ Cactus Jack Call who had died in a car accident.

Their Piper-Comanche couldn't cope with the storms and poor visibility and crashed in a woodland swamp near Camden, Tennessee. The wreckage was terrible; bodies could only be identified by fragments of clothing.

Cline's manager Randy Hughes, who was piloting the plane, and Opry stars Lloyd 'Cowboy' Copas and Hawkshaw Hawkins were also killed.

Another country star, **Jack Anglin**, of the duo Johnny And Jack, was killed in a car accident on the way to a memorial service for Cline and the band on March 7th 1963.

Three members of **Lynyrd Skynyrd** and their tour manager, Dean Kilpatrick, were killed when their chartered plane crashed in a Mississippi swamp on October 20th 1977: guitarist **Ronnie Van Zant** (29), guitarist **Steven Gaines** (28) and singer **Cassie Gaines** (29).

They were flying from Greenville, South Carolina to their next gig at Louisiana State University in Baton Rouge. Ironically, the band had been planning to buy a Lear jet to replace their older Convair 240.

Engine failure forced the crew to attempt to switch fuel to the operative wing. Instead, they accidentally dumped the fuel and, despite an attempt by the pilot to land in a clearing, the Convair crashed in a swamp near Gillsburg, Mississippi.

The deaths robbed rock of a hard-tourin', party-night band who had achieved success on a large scale with classics like Freebird and Sweet Home Alabama. Survivors Gary Rossington and Allen Collins several years later formed a new band with other ex-Skynyrd members.

Tragedy struck Allen's life again when his wife Kathy died during a tour with the new band. Then, in 1986 Collins crashed his car near his home in Jacksonville, Florida. He was paralysed from the waist down; his girlfriend was killed. He was convicted of drunk driving and was ordered to warn his young followers of the dangers of driving while under the influence which he did when he directed a 1987 Skynyrd Tribute tour.

His paralysis affected his lungs and he contracted pneumonia. He died on January 23rd 1990 after four months in hospital. He was 37.

His grave is beside his wife Kathy's in Jacksonville, Florida. Their wedding reception in 1970 had witnessed one of the first public performances of the Skynyrd epic Freebird.

Trumpet player **Bill Chase** and three members of his band Chase (**Walter Clark, John Emma and Wally York**) died on August 12th 1974 when their chartered plane crashed because of poor weather en route to a concert at Jackson, Minnesota. Bill was 39.

He was born in to an Italian family named Chiaiese living in Massachusetts. The family changed their name to Chase when he was a youngster. He graduated from Boston in classical music before turning his skills to jazz and rock after attending a concert featuring Stan Kenton and Maynard Ferguson.

Georgia-born soul star **Otis Redding** died in a plane crash on December 10th, 1967. He was 26. Four members of his backing band, the Bar-Kays –

ROCK 'TIL YOU DROP

Ronnie Caldwell (19), Carl Cunningham (18), Phalin Jones (18) and Jimmy King (18) – and his road manager also died.

Redding's twin-engine Beechcraft was en route to a concert in Madison, Wisconsin, when it crashed into Lake Monona, Madison.

Trumpeter Ben Cauley survived.

Redding produced memorable hits such as (Sittin' On) The Dock Of The Bay, I've Been Loving You Too Long and Pain In My Heart.

Redding was a big hit on the American and European concert circuit and one of the star performers at the 1967 Monterey Festival.

Brooklyn-born singer/actress **Aaliyah Haughton** died with eight others in a plane crash on August 25th, 2001. She was 22.

The plane, returning to Miami from The Bahamas where Aaliyah had been doing a video shoot, crashed shortly after take off. Engine failure or too much baggage was reported as being the cause of the crash.

Aaliyah appeared on the soundtracks for Anastasia and Dr. Dolittle, co-starred with martial arts expert Jet Li in Romeo Must Die, and had been set to start filming The Matrix II when she died.

Philadelphia singer/song-writer **Jim Croce** was killed on September 20th 1973 in a plane crash. He was 30. His lead guitarist **Maury Muehleisen** (aged 24) was also killed when their light airplane hit a treetop at the end of the runaway at Natchitoches, Louisiana. Croce recorded acclaimed albums Time In A Bottle and You Don't Mess Around With Jim.

Guitarist with Quiet Riot and Ozzy Osbourne's band, **Randy Rhoades** died when a plane prank ended disastrously at Lakeland, Florida, on March 19th 1982. He was 26.

A Beechcraft Bonanza, hired for a joy ride, crashed into a mansion and burst into flames. The plane twice buzzed the house, where the rock group was staying, and on a third pass clipped the group's tour bus and a tree, then slammed into the two-storey home. Pilot Andrew Aycock, 36, and the group's make-up artist Rachel Youngblood, 58, also died.

Osbourne escaped uninjured from the bus. Several other group members escaped unhurt from the mansion before it was gutted by flaming gasoline from the plane.

Rhoades was voted 'Best New Guitarist by Guitar Player' magazine poll and chosen as 'England's Best Heavy Metal Guitarist' for 1981 by Sounds magazine.

Texan singer/guitarist **Stevie Ray Vaughan** died in a helicopter crash on August 27th 1990. He was 35. Three members of Eric Clapton's entourage were also killed when poor visibility caused the Bell BHT-206-B to crash into a hill near East Troy, Wisconsin. They had been touring with Clapton and others and were headed for Chicago from Alpine Valley, Wisconsin. Mourners at Vaughan's funeral in his native Dallas included Stevie Wonder, Buddy Guy and Ringo Starr.

Vaughan shot to prominence in the 1980s and could count acts like The Rolling Stones and David Bowie among his fans. Guitar Player's readers voted him 'Best New Talent', 'Best Blues Album', and 'Best Electric Blues Guitarist' in 1983. The following year he won a Grammy: 'Best Traditional Blues Recording' for Texas Flood.

He battled the demons of drink and drugs and doctors warned him against continuing to mix cocaine with his whiskey shortly before he entered a London rehab clinic in 1986. He recovered to collect more awards, make more acclaimed albums and even perform at President George Bush's inauguration in 1989.

Jane Dornacker, actress, singer, comedienne and radio presenter, died in a helicopter crash on October 22nd 1986. She was 39. She was killed while doing a live traffic broadcast for WNBC over New York.

The chopper crashed from a height of 75 feet into a fence and fell into the Hudson River. She died on the way to the hospital. The pilot survived.

Dornacker had survived a crash earlier that year.

As a singer in San Francisco in the 1970s she had performed and composed with The Tubes and her all-girl band Leila and the Snakes.

American singer **Melanie Thornton** died when a plane crashed near Zurich on November 24th 2001. She was 34. Thornton, from Charleston, South Carolina, was touring to promote her album Ready To Fly. She had previously sung with the hit-selling band La Bouche.

Ten of the 33 passengers and crew on board the Crossair flight from Berlin to Zurich survived the crash, which was blamed on snow and poor visibility. But among the dead were two members of Passion Fruit - a female dance-music trio based in Germany. **Maria Serrano-Serrano** and **Nathaly van het Ende** were both 27.

Canadian folk singer **Stan Rogers** died in a fire onboard an aircraft on June 2nd 1983. He was 33.

Rogers was returning home to Ontario from the Kerrville Folk Festival in Texas when a fire started in the toilet of an Air Canada jet. It managed to land in Cincinatti but 23 people died of smoke inhalation.

Dean Martin's son **Dino Martin** was killed when the Air National Guard jet he was piloting crashed in California's San Bernardino Mountains on March 21st 1987. He was 35.

Martin, member of '60s group Dino, Desi and Billy, was on a routine training flight (he was a captain in the California Air National Guard). Air rescue took four days to locate the wreckage and the bodies of Martin and his co-pilot. Crash investigators discovered the F-4C flew upside down into the granite wall at an estimated 560 mph. Pilot disorientation was blamed.

Seven members of Oklahoma country singer Reba McEntire's band were among ten people killed in plane crash near San Diego on March 16th 1991. **Chris Austin, Kirk Capello, Joey Cigainero, Paula Kaye Evans, Terry Jackson, Michael Thomas and Tony Saputo** plus McEntire's road manager, Jim Hammon, were killed when the chartered jet crashed into a mountain two minutes after take-off. They were heading for a show in Fort Wayne, Indiana. Crew/pilot error was blamed.

A second aircraft, carrying more members of the touring entourage, took off three minutes later and heard of the tragedy when they landed in Memphis for refueling.

McEntire and her husband had decided to stay overnight in San Diego.

Rick Nelson (aged 45) and several members of his band – keyboardist **Andy Chapin** (33), drummer **Rick Intveld** (22), guitarist **Bobby Neal** (38) and bassist **Patrick Woodward** (37) – were killed on New Year's Eve 1985 when their plane crashed in Texas.

The DC-3 (previously owned by Jerry Lee Lewis) was heading to a show in Dallas when it crash-landed in a field near DeKalb. The burning plane trapped its passengers inside, killing all aboard, except the pilot and co-pilot, who escaped through the cockpit window. A faulty gas heater was blamed.

The road has claimed its fair share of victims.

Duane Allman was killed in a motorcycle accident in Macon, Georgia on October 29th 1971. He was 24.

The Nashville-born guitarist featured on works by Wilson Pickett, Aretha Franklin and Boz Scaggs before forming the Allman Brothers Band in Florida with his younger brother, Gregg. Duane played with Eric Clapton on the Derek And The Dominos' album Layla And Other Assorted Love Songs.

He died while recording the Eat A Peach album with the Allmans. He crashed his Harley-Davidson while trying to avoid colliding with a lorry and died following surgery.

Slide guitar was Duane's speciality. Their biggest critical success was the album Live at Fillmore East.

The band stumbled on after Duane's death, but on November 11th 1972 bassist **Berry Oakley** was killed in a motorcycle crash, just three blocks from the site of Duane's fatal accident. Berry was 24.

Berry's bike had collided with a bus but he insisted he did not need treat-

-ment for his injuries. Soon afterwards he became delirious and fell into a coma. He was taken to hospital where he died of a fractured skull and brain haemorrhage - less than two hours after the crash.

Gregg (married to Cher and spending much of his time in Hollywood) was having drug problems. The band split in 1976 after Gregg avoided jail by informing on former road manager Scooter Herring for drug dealing.

Lamar Williams, who had replaced Oakley on bass, died from cancer in Los Angeles on January 25th 1983. He was 34. Williams had served in Vietnam and been exposed to Agent Orange – a herbicide used to destroy crops which provided cover for Viet Cong forces.

Lead singer with San Francisco band Vicious Rumors, **Carl 'The Voice' Albert** died on April 23rd 1995 following a car crash while returning from rehearsals. He was 33. The car had careered off the road and rammed into a tree.

Memphis-born **Chris Bell**, lead singer with Big Star, died when his car crashed into a telephone pole on December 27th, 1978. He was 27.

Bell made one album with Big Star before leaving the band. He performed sporadically as a solo artist. Demos recorded in France shortly before his death were remastered and released in 1992 as I Am The Cosmos.

Three members of the British glam-rock pioneers T-Rex died in their 30s.

Singer-songwriter **Marc Bolan** was killed in a car crash on September 16th 1977. He was 30.

Bolan (born Mark Feld in Hackney, London) died when a car hit a tree on a London road. His partner, former backing singer Gloria Jones, was driving and survived the accident.

A hospital worker stole the clothes Bolan was wearing and attempted to sell them to fans. Bolan's home was ransacked the day after his death by fans hunting souvenirs (or profit).

Bolan never made it big in the USA but lived there for a while to avoid the heavy UK tax system. He developed too strong a liking for drink and cocaine before returning home to try and resurrect a career that had yielded a string of UK number ones in the early 70s.

He landed his own TV show which would introduce Billy Idol and the Boomtown Rats to a wider audience. His last show featured a duet with David Bowie - a long-time friendly rival.

Percussionist/singer **Steve Took** (Stephen Ross Porter), who formed the original band, Tyrannosaurus Rex by answering an advert Bolan had placed in a newspaper, choked to death on October 27th 1980. He was 31.

He had been taking drugs with girlfriend Valerie Billet in their London flat and died of asphyxiation when a cocktail cherry became blocked. Bass player **Steve Currie**, who also joined the band after seeing an advert, died in a car crash in Portugal on April 28th 1981. He was 34. After leaving T-Rex in 1976 Currie returned to his hometown of Grimsby and played with Chris Spedding's band.

Jamaican reggae star with Inner Circle, **Jacob Miller** died on the Caribbean island when his car struck a telephone pole on March 23rd 1980. He was 26.

Miller was a charismatic, lively performer who did much to heighten awareness of Jamaica's problems through his music. Inner Circle had been scheduled to go on tour with Bob Marley when Miller died.

Byrds guitarist **Clarence White** was killed by a drunk driver on July 14th 1973 while he and his two brothers were loading equipment after a concert in Lancaster, California. He was 29.

White had been a performer since a young child and gained a wide reputation for his innovative guitar work from the bluegrass with The Kentucky Colonels to the electric country rock with Gram Parsons and The Byrds.

Parsons sang at his funeral and was himself to die two months later from an overdose.

Country singer **Amie Comeaux** was killed in a car crash on December 21st 1997. She was 21.

She died when her Dodge Avenger skidded and rammed into a tree near Lacombe, Louisiana. She was driving her grandmother and godchild home from a family gathering in Alabama. Both passengers survived.

Eldon Hoke (aka El Duce) was killed by a train in Riverside, California, on April 19th 1997. He was 39. He had performed at a Los Angeles bar the previous night.

Drummer and vocalist with The Mentors, Hoke was drunk when he stumbled into the path of the train. He and The Mentors achieved notoriety in 1985 when a US Senate hearings branded Mentors' lyrics the most obscene in music. Hoke, born in Seattle, later claimed he had been approached to kill Kurt Cobain.

American singer **Jesse Belvin,** his wife Jo Ann and their driver died in a car crash at Hope, Arkansas, on February 6th 1960. He was 27. Belvin, who co-wrote The Penguins' Earth Angel and whose hit single Goodnight My Love closed a popular American radio show, was returning from performing the first show in Little Rock before an integrated audience.

The show caused a storm. Belvin, touted by some as The Black Elvis, incensed white supremacist groups. He had received numerous death threats, and his show was halted twice by groups looking for trouble and urging whites in the crowd to walk out. Police who attended the accident scene reported that both rear tyres appeared to have been tampered with.

Jazz trumpeter **Clifford Brown** and pianist **Richie Powell** died in a car accident on June 26th 1956. Both men were 25. Powell's wife, Nancy, was driving the car and was also killed when she lost control in a skid and it hurtled down an 18-foot embankment in Bedford, Pennsylvania. They were heading from Philadelphia to perform with Max Roach in Chicago.

Milton Brown, the 'Founder of Western Swing', died on April 18th 1936 following a car accident in Fort Worth, Texas. He was 32.

Brown and a 16-year-old passenger, Katherine Prehoditch, were driving home when the crash happened. The girl was killed instantly but Brown lingered on for five days in hospital before succumbing to 'traumatic pneumonia'.

Bianca Butthole (born Bianca Halstead), singer and bass player with Hollywood bitch rockers Betty Blowtorch, died in a car crash near New Orleans on December 15th 2001. She was 36.

After a show with tour mates Nashville Pussy, Bianca went for an early morning drive in a friend's Corvette. His car spun round as he lost control and it was hit by another car on the passenger side. There were no other fatalities.

Billy Stewart and three members of his band The Soul Kings died when their car plummeted off a bridge and into a river in Smithfield, North Carolina, on January 17th 1970. Stewart was 32.

Also killed in the accident were: band members Norman Pedro Rich, William Cathey and Rico Hightower. The Soul Kings enjoyed top ten success in the USA with Summertime and Sitting In The Park in the mid-60s.

Singer/pianist **Earl Grant** died in a car accident in Lordsburg, New Mexico, on June 10th 1970. He was 37. Grant was returning from a performance in Juarez, Mexico.

British DJ **Kemistry** (Kemi Olusanya) died in a freak traffic accident on April 25th 1999. She was 35. Kemistry and Storm (her DJ partner) were travelling on the M3 near Winchester after a performance in Southampton when a 10-pound marker was flicked up by another vehicle and smashed through the windscreen. Kemistry was killed instantly.

Kemistry and Storm were a rare female DJ act who helped launch the Metalheadz label.

Criss Oliva, guitar player with Florida metal band Savatage, died in a car crash on October 17th 1993. He was 30. Oliva was killed instantly and his wife, Dawn, suffered serious injuries when their Mazda was hit by a car as they were traveling to the Livestock Festival in Zephyrhills, Florida.

The driver of the other car was three times over the drink-driving limit.

He had six previous convictions for drink-driving.

Doreen Waddell, former singer with Soul II Soul and The KLF, died after being hit by three cars in Shoreham, West Sussex, on March 1st 2002. She was 36. Waddell had dashed out of a Tesco store's rear exit and was being pursued by store detectives after being accused of shop-lifting. Her injuries were so bad that it was several days before she was identified – from her fingerprints.

Jerry Wick, guitarist and lead singer for the Columbus, Ohio rock band Gaunt, was killed while riding his bike at 2.30am on January 10th 2001. He was 33. Brian Jenkins was given three years' probation for fleeing the accident. Jenkins, 27, was banned from driving for six months except to go to work, and was ordered to perform 120 hours of community service with Mothers Against Drunk Driving.

Jenkins claimed he didn't know he had hit a person but said people had pelted his Ford Escort and broken its windshield. Wick's father said. "If I was hit by a brick, I would've reported it right away. A brick weighs 10 pounds. My boy weighed 165 pounds, plus the bike - another 35. That's like hitting a brick wall."

Prosecuting attorney Bob Krapenc said Jenkins's girlfriend called 911 after the crash and said that she and Jenkins may have seen a body at the intersection but didn't mention hitting someone. It later was discovered that she wasn't with Jenkins at the time.

Jenkins was charged with fleeing but not with intentionally hitting Wick, who had been riding his bicycle and holding a box of pizza - all while his blood-alcohol level was 0.26 percent, more than twice the level at which someone is considered to be drunk in Ohio.

O'Neill said that because Jenkins fled, investigators were unable to determine whether or not he also had been drinking.

Multi-instrumentalist **Mary Hansen** from the group Stereolab was killed when a car knocked her off her bicycle in London on December 9th 2002. She was 36. Hansen was buried in her home city of Brisbane, Australia.

Metallica bassist **Cliff Burton** was killed on September 27th 1986 when the band's tour bus crashed and he was thrown out of the window. He was 24. The band and crew were travelling on two buses from Stockholm to Copenhagen. The bus carrying the band suddenly skidded on black ice, swerved and careered down the wrong side of the road.

It was around 5am and the violence of the movements woke the band members. The bus slid to a halt and rolled over by the side of the road near the village of Ljungby, Sweden.

Most managed to scramble free from the wreckage with minor injuries;

two were trapped for several hours before being rescued by firemen. Burton, however, had been crushed to death the moment the bus rolled over.

Drummer with British folk-rock group Fairport Convention, **Martin Lamble** died in an accident on the M1 motorway on May 12th 1969. He was 19. The band's driver fell asleep and the van tumbled over an embankment. The crash also claimed the life of guitarist Richard Thompson's girlfriend Jeannie Franklyn. The driver went through the windscreen, breaking both his legs. Other band members suffered various injuries.

Guitarist with Canadian band Helix, **Paul Hackman** died when their tour bus crashed on July 5th 1992. He was 39.

The bus plunged down a 40-foot cliff near Kamloops, British Columbia. Founder member Hackman was killed, two roadies suffered serious injuries and others minor scrapes.

Helix's seven albums sold well and they broke out of the Canadian circuit by going on tour with groups such as Kiss, Motorhead and Aerosmith.

For Squirrels' singer **Jack Vigliatura** (aged 21), bass player **Bill White** (23) and tour manager **Tim Bender** (23) were killed on September 8th 1995 when their van overturned on a Georgia road.

The Florida band were heading home from a gig at CBGB's in New York when a tyre blew out on Inter-state 95. Jack Griego, drummer with For Squirrels, suffered a broken back and guitarist Travis Michael Tooke broke an elbow.

Lead singer and guitarist with Californian New Wave band The Minutemen, **Dennes Boon** was killed in a car accident on December 22nd 1985 near Tucson, Arizona. He was 27.

Boon was asleep in the van when its axle broke and he was thrown out.

Bluesman **Duster Bennett** died in a car accident on March 26th 1976. He was 29. Bennett, who played with many artists including Fleetwood Mac and The Bluesbreakers, fell asleep at the wheel of his car while returning home from a gig in the Midlands.

Californian rock 'n roller **Eddie Cochran** (Edward Ray Cochran) died on April 17th 1960 in a road accident. He was 21.

Cochran had several hits in the late 50s. Classics such as Summertime Blues and C'mon Everybody would live long after his death.

The fatal accident occurred after a successful UK tour with Gene Vincent had ended at Bristol's Hippodrome. Cochran, Vincent plus Sharon Sheeley and Patrick Thomkins hired a cab to take them to London. Cochran had booked a flight home for Easter Sunday.

George Martin, the driver of the Ford Consul, took a wrong turn near the

Wiltshire town of Chippenham, lost control, careered for 50 yards and crashed. It was just before midnight on April 16th. All were taken to a local hospital and then to St Martin's in Bath. Cochran died from brain injuries in the afternoon of April 17th.

Martin was later convicted of causing Cochran's death by dangerous driving. He was banned for 15 years and fined fifty pounds.

Greg Arama, bassist with the Amboy Dukes, was killed when he drove his motorbike over a cliff in California on September 18th, 1979. He was 29. Arama had been in Detroit's Amboy Dukes when they launched 'Motor City Madman' guitarist Ted Nugent to fame. Nugent claimed heroin took over Arama and he had to fire him from the band.

New York singer/song-writer **Harry Chapin** was killed in a car crash on July 16th 1981. He was 38.

His Volkswagen, with emergency lights flashing as he switched lanes, was hit from behind by a tractor-trailer on the Long Island Expressway. The crash caused Chapin's fuel tank to catch fire. Truck driver Robert Eggleton suffered burns on his face and arms as he dragged Chapin free. Chapin died from the impact and not from his minor burns.

Chapin, born in New York's musical hotbed of Greenwich Village, had an easy-listening style and produced hits such as Taxi and W.O.L.D.

He backed many charities and local causes, performing many benefit concerts. He was en route to a free concert when he died.

Johnny Kidd, one of the first British rock 'n roll stars, was killed in a car accident in Radcliffe, Lancashire on October 7th 1966. He was 27.

He was born Frederick Heath in London and shot to fame with his band The Pirates during the early 60s explosion of beat music. Their most memorable hit was the classic Shakin' All Over. Kidd told an interviewer:

"When I was going round with a bunch of lads and we happened to see a girl who was a real sizzler we used to say that she gave us 'quivers down the membranes'...this more than anything inspired me to write Shakin' All Over."

Grateful Dead keyboard player **Keith Godchaux** died in a car accident in Marin County, California on July 23rd 1980. He was 32. He was married to Donna (born Donna Jean Thatcher) who sang with the Dead for a spell. Keith's drug problems caused them to leave the Dead in 1979.

Lisa 'Left Eye' Lopes, member of hip-hop group TLC, was killed in a motor accident on April 26th 2002 in Honduras. She was 30. The head-on collision on a treacherous two-lane country road occurred shortly before 6 p.m. outside La Ceiba, a town on the Atlantic coast. Lopes, who was driving, died instantly.

The singer was one of eight people in the vehicle – three members of the band Egypt needed hospital treatment. Lopes had a UK number one, duetting with Spice Girl Melanie C on Never Be the Same Again in 2000.

Singer/song-writer with Californian band Snot, **Lynn Strait** died on December 11th 1998 in a car crash near Santa Barbara. He was 30.

Strait's dog, Dobbs, who graced the cover of the band's 1997 debut album Get Some, was also killed. Strait was arrested at an OzzFest show in 1997 in Mansfield, Massachusetts.

He was reported to have appeared onstage naked for a dare and engaged in oral sex with a dancer that was part of Limp Bizkit's stage show. Court charges were pending when he died.

Drummer with punk band Hanoi Rocks, **Nicholas 'Razzle' Dingley** was killed in a car accident in Redondo Beach, California on December 8th 1984. He was 24.

Hanoi band members had been partying at the beach home of Motley Crue singer Vince Neil. Razzle decided to join Neil on a beer run despite the singer being over the limit.

Neil lost control of his Ford Pantera as he rounded a parked fire truck close to his home. He ended up on the opposite side of the road, leaving the driver of a Volkswagen with brain damage and Razzle dead.

Razzle's body was flown back to his Isle Of Wight village for cremation. Neil was sentenced to 30 days jail and ordered to pay $2.6m in compensation to the accident victims.

Trinidad-born drummer with British New Wave band Echo & The Bunnymen, **Pete DeFreitas** was killed on June 14th 1989 in a motorcycle accident in Rugeley while driving to rehearsals. He was 27.

American folk singer **Richard Farina** died in a motorcycle accident in California on April 30th 1966. He was 29.

Farina had been excited at spotting a new Harley Davidson Sportster at a friend's house in Carmel, California. He asked the owner, Willie Hinds, to take him for a ride. Police estimated the bike must have been clocking 90mph round a bend on Carmel Valley Road when Farina was thrown off and smashed his head against some rocks, dying almost instantly. Hinds had cuts to his arms and head.

Farina had been celebrating the publication of his novel Been Down So Long It Looks Like Up To Me.

Charlatans keyboard player **Rob Collins** died on his way to hospital in the early hours of July 23rd 1996 following a drunk-driving accident the previous night. He was 33.

Collins had a troubled past, being convicted for being drunk and disorderly and serving eight months in jail for acting as getaway driver in an armed robbery. He had been drinking before getting into his BMW to drive to Rockfield Studios in Gwent for a recording session. He lost control of the car on a country road and was thrown 50ft.

Irreverent comedian/crooner **Sam Kinison** was killed by a teenaged drunk driver on April 10th 1992. He was 38.

Born into a preacher's family in Yakima, Washington, Kinison earned a reputation as one of the loudest and rudest acts of the 1980s.

Major league rock stars would appear in his music videos and attend his concerts. He had tried to kick drink and drugs when he married Malika Souiri – his third wife. The new couple were on their way to a show in Laughlin, Nevada, when their car was hit head-on. Malika survived.

During his last concert tour he told one audience: "Folks, I've been straight for seventeen days… (crowd jeers)…Not all in a row."

Ohio punkster **Stiv Bators**, lead singer for The Dead Boys, was killed on June 4th 1990 after being hit by a car in Paris. He was 39. The Dead Boys were a wild bunch: "Fuck art, let's rock!" was their motto.

The Dead Boys disbanded in 1979, shortly after the almost-fatal stabbing of their drummer Johnny Blitz. Bators worked as a solo artist and in several bands, including The Lords Of The New Church which he formed in 1981.

At one gig with The Lords in 1983, Bators' stage act of hanging himself with his microphone wire backfired. An alert roadie noticed he was turning blue. He was taken to hospital and later informed that for a few minutes he had actually been clinically dead.

He was working on a new recording in Paris when he met his death. He was able to walk home after being struck by a car while he was standing on a pavement but he died that evening in his sleep.

Tommy Caldwell, bass player with southern rockers the Marshall Tucker Band, died on April 28th 1980 from injuries sustained in a car accident a week earlier near his home in Spartanburg, South Carolina. He was 30.

Los Angeles-born bass player **Rushton Moreve**, who had a brief stint with rockers Steppenwolf, died in a car accident in his home city on July 1st 1981. He was 33.

Tim 'Bone' Kelly, guitarist with heavy metal band Slaughter, was killed on February 5th, 1998 when his car was hit head-on by a giant tractor-trailer in Bagdad, Arizona. He was 34.

Brainiac singer **Tim Taylor** was killed in a car accident in the early hours of May 23rd 1997 while driving from the studio to his Dayton, Ohio home. He was 28.

ROCK 'TIL YOU DROP

Roger Patterson, bass player with American metal band Atheist, died in a motor accident while returning from a tour on February 16th 1991. He was 22.

Les Kummel, bass player with The New Colony Six, died in a car crash in Chicago on December 18th 1978. He was 33.

John Scott Rogers (aka Rip Thrillby), leader of Atlanta band The Penetrators, died in a car crash on May 11th 2003. He was 36.

He was killed after being thrown out of a friend's car and sent hurtling over a bridge.

Count Bishops guitarist **Zenon de Fleur** died in surgery on March 17th 1979 – a week after being involved in a car crash. He was 28.

Born Zenon Hierowski, he had been seriously injured in a car accident during the early hours of March 10th after a Bishops gig at The Nashville in West London. He had been in intensive care at West Middlesex Hospital, Brentford, but had been taken off the critical list. He had been conscious and even asked to see proofs of the artwork for the Bishops third album which had just been completed.

He complained of having trouble breathing, and what was expected to be a fairly routine operation ended with him dying on the operating table.

Merle Watson, son of folk singer Doc Watson, was killed in a freak accident when he was hurled from a tractor at his farm in Lenoir, North Carolina, on October 23rd 1985. He was 36.

He had been doing some carpentry when a piece of wood became embedded in his arm. A neighbour provided medical attention but Watson, weak from loss of blood, drove his tractor over an embankment. The tractor landed on top of him.

Yardbirds vocalist **Keith Relf** electrocuted himself while playing guitar in his bath at his London home on May 14th 1976. He was 33. The Yardbirds were famous for launching the careers of guitar greats Eric Clapton, Jimmy Page and Jeff Beck. After the group disbanded in the late 60s, Relf performed with Renaissance, Medicine Head and Armageddon.

Stone The Crows guitarist **Leslie Harvey** was electrocuted on stage before a concert in Swansea on May 3rd 1972. He was 27. Harvey, younger brother of the 'Sensational' Alex Harvey, touched a mic and his guitar at the same time during a soundcheck at the Top Rank Ballroom. The band never recovered from his death and split the following year.

French rock singer **Claude Francois** (Clo-Clo) was electrocuted in his shower on March 11th 1978. He was 39.

Clo-Clo was a huge star in France; his shows were accompanied by Beatles-style hysteria; he was invited to dine with the president (Giscard

D'Estaing). His death so stunned his fans that two of them committed suicide. He died in his Paris appartment when he tried to change a light bulb.

Shadows bass guitarist **John Henry Rostill** died in his home studio on November 26th, 1973. He was 31. He had been electrocuted and his body was discovered by his wife Margaret.

Birmingham-born Rostill had been with The Shadows from November 1963 to the break-up in December 1968. He later toured the USA with Tom Jones and wrote several songs, which were recorded by the likes of Olivia Newton John.

Ken Jensen, drummer with Canadian punks D.O.A., died in a fire at his Vancouver home on January 28th 1995. He was 29. "A seven dollar smoke detector would have saved his life," said a fireman. Four people escaped the blaze, which was believed to have been caused by a cigarette.

Yugoslav-born composer producer **Suba** (born Mitar Subotic) was killed in a studio fire on November 2nd 1999. He was 38. After being rescued from the fire, Suba had re-entered the room to recover tapes for an album he was working on. He was overcome and died in hospital from smoke asphyxiation.

He made hi-tech music for a host of performers and outlets. Including 15 movies and TV companies in Yugoslavia, France and Brazil.

A terrible fire swept through The Station nightclub in West Warwick, Rhode Island on February 20th 2003 when pyrotechnics used by band Great White shot sparks toward the ceiling and ignited the roof and walls. Within minutes the fire had caused the roof to collapse.

The inferno claimed 100 lives and left more than 200 injured.

Calls to West Warwick police capture the panic. "We have multiple people trapped. We're dragging them out one by one," an officer shouted over his emergency radio to the West Warwick Police Department dispatcher. "We have people on fire inside."

Club officials said the special effects were used without permission. Singer Jack Russell said the band's manager checked with the club before the show and the use of pyrotechnics was approved.

Ty Longley, guitar player with Great White, was among the dead. He was 32. His girlfriend, Heidi, was two months pregnant. She later gave birth to a son, Acey.

Jamaican reggae singer **Garnett Silk** was killed on December 9th 1994 when a propane tank at his home exploded. He was 28.

Silk, once hailed as a worthy successor to Bob Marley, had borrowed two guns from his lawyer, following a burglary at his home. Someone was showing Silk how to use one of the guns when it went off. The bullet hit a gas tank and the resulting explosion killed Silk and his mother, and severely burned two of his brothers.

Founder member of The Rolling Stones, **Brian Jones** drowned on July 3rd 1969. He was 27. Jones had been kicked out of the band earlier that summer due to his increasing drug-dependency.

Born Lewis Brian Hopkin-Jones in Cheltenham, he was one of the original bad boys of rock. While still at school Jones made two local people pregnant - a 14-year-old girl and a married woman. He speedily switched from a likeable lad to a social outcast.

Though Jones never married, he would father children by at least three other women. He soon left the polite circles of Cheltenham headed for London and hooked up with Mick Jagger and Keith Richards in 1962 to form what would develop into the Greatest Rock 'n Roll Band In The World.

The Stones were rougher and more rebellious than The Beatles – an image they didn't have to work on.

Jones was musically the most adventurous of the band, testing out a variety of instruments including dulcimer and sitar. He was also, tragically, adventurous socially. He couldn't keep his hands off drink, drugs or girls. Despite being the main thrust behind the band's launch, he lost power to the Jagger-Richards song-writing team. His drug-intake increased to match his paranoia. He fell foul of the law in 1967. His London flat was raided on May 11th 1967 - the day Jagger and Richards appeared in court over the infamous Redlands bust (the pair were jailed but released on appeal).

When his case came to trial in October, Jones pleaded guilty to possession of cannabis and permitting his premises to be used for the smoking of cannabis. He was sentenced to nine months but released on bail after one night in Wormwood Scrubs. A psychiatrist told the December appeal hearing that Jones's mental state was precarious and that he had a "fragile grasp of reality". He escaped jail.

He had another lucky escape the following summer following another raid. He told the court that the drugs had been planted and he was let off with another fine.

His influence in the band was becoming less and less, his mental state making him a handicap at recording sessions. Too depressed, drunk or high to contribute. His input would be over-recorded while he often slept.

The end came in June 1969 – his popularity with fans had kept him in the band this long. "I no longer see eye to eye with the others over the discs we are cutting," read a Press release.

Jones did have musical projects to turn to, plus he was restoring his new home in Sussex - Cotchford Farm (where Winnie The Pooh was penned by A. A. Milne.) It was here that his body was discovered at the bottom of a swimming pool early on July 3rd 1969.

An inquest was held and the coroner proclaimed: "Death by misadventure, cause of death drowning". Not murder nor suicide as books continued to claim decades after the event - just a sad end to a life that experienced triumph and tragedy in almost equal measure.

Jagger said: "I am wordless, sad and shocked. Something has gone. We were like a pack, like a family, we Stones. I just say my prayers for him. I hope he becomes blessed. I hope he is finding peace; I really want him to."

A few days later Jagger's girlfriend Marianne Faithfull would attempt suicide. Jones was buried in his hometown of Cheltenham.

A free concert at Hyde Park, originally intended as a launchpad for new guitarist Mick Taylor, turned into a tribute for Jones as Jagger opened the show with a eulogy – Adonis by Shelley.

On the 30th anniversary of Jones's death, Who guitarist Pete Townshend told Mojo magazine: "When we played The Rolling Stones' Rock And Roll Circus I was very upset about Brian's condition. I was upset about Keith Richards' green complexion, too, but he seemed in good spirits.

"Brian was defeated. I took Mick and Keith aside and they were quite frank about it all. They said Brian had ceased to function, they were afraid he would slip away.

"They certainly were not hard-nosed about him. But they were determined not to let him drag them down, that was clear. Brian certainly slipped away that evening. He died soon after.

"I was melodramatically upset when he died. He was the first friend of mine that had ever died. He was the first person I knew well in my business that died. It seemed to me to be a portent and thus it proved to be. I wrote a really crap song for him, Normal Day for Brian. He deserved better and one day he will get it."

Beach Boy **Dennis Wilson** (he was one who decided they should do surfing songs) drowned on December 28th 1983. He was 39.

Dennis led a troubled life, fighting the demons brought on by drink and drugs and his friendship with mass murderer Charles Manson. Dennis would be in and out of rehab for most of his career. He had been drinking the previous night and started again early on the morning of his death.

He was on a friend's yacht at the Marina Del Rey, Los Angeles and despite the cold decided to go for a swim. Divers fished his body out after alarmed friends contacted them. Wilson's wish was granted and he was buried at sea.

Jeff Buckley drowned in the Mississippi near Memphis on May 29th

1997. He was 30. His father, Tim Buckley, died of a drug overdose in 1975. He had left Jeff's mum before he was born.

Jeff was born in Orange County, California and made his name in New York as a talented writer/performer. He had performed a solo show a few nights before his death and was due to join his bandmates to rehearse new material he had been finishing in Memphis. The last time he was seen alive he was swimming on his back, fully-clothed and singing.

Motown artist **Shorty Long** drowned in a boating accident with friend Oscar Williams on the Detroit River on June 29th 1969. He was 29.

Frederick Earl Long was nicknamed Shorty due to his diminutive stature. He was just over five feet tall. His biggest hit was Here Comes The Judge, which reached Number Five in the Billboard charts.

Will Sin (William Sinnott), bass player with Scottish band The Shamen, drowned off Gomera in the Canary Islands on May 23rd 1991. He was 31. The Shamen had been shooting a video in Gomera.

Johnny Burnette, a 1950s singer who attended the same school as Elvis, drowned after falling from his boat while fishing on Clear Lake, California, on August 1st 1964. He was 30.

Rhythm and blues star **Johnny Ace** killed himself while playing Russian roulette on Christmas Day in Houston 1954. He was 25.

Ace, born John Alexander, had gone backstage for a five-minute break and had been fooling around with a revolver with one bullet in the chamber.

New York-based **Bobby Bloom** accidentally shot himself (some say suicide) on February 28th 1974. He was 28. He enjoyed a transatlantic hit with Montego Bay and wrote for many 1960s artists, including The Monkees.

Terry Kath, vocalist and guitar player with Chicago, died when he shot himself in a prank on January 23rd 1978. He was 31.

Kath was cleaning two guns at roadie Donnie Johnson's home – a .38 pistol and a nine millimeter gun. "Don't worry it's not loaded," Kath told Johnson before shooting himself in the head. The Los Angeles coroner recorded a verdict of "accidental gunshot wound to the head under the influence of alcohol and drugs." Kath had a huge fan club, including Jimi Hendrix who told Chicago saxophone player Walter Parazaider: "Your guitar player is better than me."

Teemu 'Somnium' Raimoranta, guitarist with Finnish rock band Finntroll, died on March 16th 2003. He was 25. Raimoranta fell while drunk from a bridge in Helsinki.

Bass player with several Californian groups (The Vejtables, The Wilde Knights) in the 60s and early 70s, **Rick Dey** died on November 5th 1973 after inhaling laughing gas at a Hollywood party. He was 25.

DRUGS

EVEN Mozart wasn't immune to the musicians' curses. He died in Vienna from an infection on December 5th, 1791, his body weakened by alcoholism and syphilis. He may have actually overdosed in an attempt to cure his syphilis. He was 35.

Modern musicians seem particularly prone to taking lethal substances. Sports stars take illegal substances in the pursuit of fool's gold, conning themselves and their fans that they have ACHIEVED the pinnacle.

Music-makers turn to drink and drugs to get high, obviously; to escape, sometimes; to create, often. Many a classic album owes its essence to the muse Amphetamina.

The hardy ones – or just plain lucky ones - manage to pull themselves back from the brink of destruction, with the help of friends and a sturdy dose of self-discipline. It took the leniency of a Toronto judge to persuade Rolling Stones guitarist Keith Richards that his luck, with the law as well as his health, was running out.

Stones former manager Andrew Loog Oldham can't believe he survived his 1960s dietary habits – drugs for starters, drugs for main course, drugs for dessert. The occasional solid was partaken as an afterthought to line the insides.

A clutch of stars, however, failed to join Mozart in reaching the grand old age of 35. Twenty-seven was a good age to die, it appears. Farewell to Jimi Hendrix, Jim Morrison, Janis Joplin, Kurt Cobain and a good few others.

The deaths of Hendrix and Cobain gave Seattle's tourist industry a shot in the arm, so to speak.

Both rock legends hailed from Washington State — Hendrix was born in Seattle and Cobain 90 miles south-west in Hoquaim.

Both were laid to rest in Seattle in one way or another.

Fans and curious tourists still flock to Hendrix's grave at the Greenwood Memorial - a quarter of a century after the death of rock's most famous and acclaimed guitarist. Grunge king Cobain had a mixed up death in fitting with his mixed up life. His widow, Courtney Love, is believed to have scattered some of his ashes in a river, stuffed some inside a doll and had the others made into clay ornaments by Buddhist monks. She claimed local authorities either refused to house his remains or required extortionate sums to oblige.

His house and other Seattle haunts frequented by Cobain provide focal points for the pilgrims.

Jimi Hendrix: he spent his first four years as Johnny Allen Hendrix before his father changed it to James Marshall Hendrix. The rock world knew him as Jimi – a guitar player like none before him and few after. He died in London on September 18th 1970 from drug-related asphyxia. He was 27.

Hendrix flew to England on August 27th 1970 with his new band City Of Love which had been formed earlier in the year from the remnants of Jimi Hendrix Experience.

Three days later they headlined the Isle Of Wight festival. Two poorly-performed and less well-received festival appearances – in Denmark and Germany – followed before Hendrix returned to London.

He jammed with Eric Burdon at Ronnie Scott's club in London – his final live appearance on September 16th – and was dead within 48 hours.

An inquest was held in London and the coroner instructed the jury to return an open verdict. Cause of death was given as "inhalation of vomit due to barbiturate intoxication".

Some biographers claimed American agencies lay in the shadows and that Hendrix's death may not have been as accidental as it seemed.

Friends cited the behaviour of Hendrix's manager Mike Jeffrey – a Londoner who had worked in intelligence circles – as a reason for the star's paranoia.

Monika Danneman, Hendrix's fiancée, said he so mistrusted his manager that he was seeking ways to end their contract. He blamed Jeffrey for a Toronto heroin bust in 1969, for mismanaging/abusing the Jimi Hendrix Experience's finances and for attempting to control his career and his life. Dannemann was with Hendrix when he died at the Samarkand Hotel.

Hendrix suffered from insomnia and Dannemann had seen him take some sleeping tablets before she went to bed at 3am. The next morning she went to buy some cigarettes and returned to find the star in a bad way. She phoned a friend and then dialled 999. She claimed Hendrix was still alive when the paramedics arrived. The paramedics claim he was dead and there was no-one else in the flat.

"Hendrix had been dead for hours rather than minutes when he was admitted to the hospital," the doctor who examined him told The Times.

Investigators down the years have tried to prove that Hendrix was murdered by The Mob or the CIA; and that he probably drowned by having red wine forced down him.

His manager Jeffrey later died of suspicious circumstances when the plane conveying him to London on Hendrix Estate business blew up over France.

Kurt Cobain: The Nirvana leader shot himself at his Seattle home on April 5th 1994. He was 27. He left behind a huge following. Nirvana's Nevermind album sold more than ten-million copies around the world and Cobain was hailed as the spokesman of the 90s generation.

The actual events surrounding his death remain clouded in mystery. The official verdict was suicide, but investigators have since claimed he was murdered. Police, alerted by an electrician, broke into his home on April 8th and found Cobain dead on the floor of the greenhouse above the garage. A shotgun lay pointed at his chin. He had been dead for some time. He had left a suicide note addressed to his fans, wife Courtney Love and their daughter Frances Bean.

The 'poet of pain' had been in a shocking state of health for some time. He had suffered excruciating stomach pains since his youth and had a painful spinal disorder.

He turned to drugs to escape physical and mental agonies. The post mortem discovered a heavy dose of heroin in his body. The month before his death Cobain had cancelled a European tour due to illness. He was in a coma for a day in Rome (medically dead, according to his doctors) after taking (or being administered) Rohypnol – the date-rape drug – mixed with champagne.

Dr. Galletta, the Rome physician, said: "Cobain doesn't know what happened to him. When he emerged from the coma, he was very hungry and asked for a strawberry milkshake!"

Cobain had been planning to divorce Love but denied trying to commit suicide in Rome. He and Love returned to Seattle on March 12th. Six days later police were called to their home when Love reported Cobain was suicidal. He denied it.

The couple continued to argue over the next few days until Love went to Los Angeles. During her absence Cobain bought a Remington shotgun and then checked into an LA rehab clinic for two days. He arrived back in Seattle just after midnight on April 2nd and was reportedly in good health, smiling and signing autographs at the airport.

Love, pretending to be Cobain's mother, Wendy, filed a missing person's report to Seattle police on April 4th. No-one is reported to have seen Cobain alive since that day. Love OD'd in LA on April 7th and was charged with drug offences after being released from hospital.

Cobain's lengthy suicide note (though of dubious legitimacy) concluded:

Thank you all from the pit of my burning, nauseous stomach for your letters and concern during the past years. I'm too much of an erratic, moody, baby! I don't have the passion anymore, and so remember, it's better to burn out than to fade away.
Peace, Love, Empathy Kurt Cobain
Frances and Courtney, I'll be at your altar. Please keep going Courtney, for Frances. For her life, which will be so much happier without me. I LOVE YOU, I LOVE YOU!

Cobain was cremated and Love dealt with his remains. According to various sources, she scattered some, buried some in their garden and around the Seattle area, and carried some around with her in a teddy bear-shaped rucksack.

She landed at the Tibetan Buddhist Namgyal Monastery in Ithaca, New York State. She and Cobain had a shared interest in Buddhism.

To prepare his soul for the next life, Love asked the monks to consecrate the ashes by moulding them into tsatsas - cone- shaped sculptures three inches tall. Not all the ashes ended up in the cones. A security guard at an airport asked her "What's that greyish powder coming out of your teddy bear?" She showed him and as some ashes fell out they were sucked into a ventilation system. "That's my husband," Love told the guard.

Two month's after Cobain's death, his friend **Kristen Pfaff** died of an overdose in her Seattle flat. Pfaff, bass player and singer with Love's band Hole, died of a drug overdose on June 16th 1994. She was 27.

Paul Erickson, a member of the group Hammerhead, discovered Pfaff's body when he forced open the bathroom. Syringes and drug paraphernalia lay by the bathtub in which she died.

Pfaff had been in rehab for five months the previous winter and friends believed she had kicked her habit. On the day her body was discovered, Pfaff had packed a van to move to Minneapolis. She was desperate to escape Love the control freak and the Seattle drug culture. She was hooking up with her old band Janitor Joe with whom she had recently been on tour.

Alice in Chains frontman **Layne Staley** was found dead in his Seattle home on April 5th 2002. He was 34.

Tests revealed he had been dead for several days. Police went to check on Staley after friends said they were concerned about his welfare and had not seen him for two weeks.

The police discovered his body surrounded by drug equipment. The body wasn't immediately identifiable as that of Staley, who had had a long battle with drugs.

Singer with legendary American band The Doors, **Jim Morrison** was found dead from a booze and heroin-induced heart attack in the bath at his Paris apartment early on the morning of July 3rd 1971. He was 27.

Morrison had become disenchanted with The Doors and the music scene following his 1970 conviction in Miami of several counts, including indecent exposure, profanity and drunkenness at a show at the Dinner Key Auditorium on March 1st 1969.

Morrison's behaviour sparked outrage across the States. Concerts were cancelled by disgusted and worried promoters, radio stations banned Doors' music. Morrison was sentenced to six months hard labour. He moved to Paris with his girlfriend Pam Courson while awaiting the appeal. He would die before that appeal could be heard.

Morrison had scored his fatal very pure fix at a Paris club the night before he died. Down the years many fans have made the pilgrimage to see Morrison's resting place at the famous Pere Lachaise cemetery, which also houses the bodies of literary giants Marcel Proust, Jean-Paul Sartre and Oscar Wilde (another who had sought refuge in Paris).

Texan blues singer **Janis Joplin** died from a heroin overdose on October 4th, 1970 in a Los Angeles hotel room. She was 27.

She had already dabbled with drugs on her travels around the country before settling in San Francisco at the height of flower power in 1966.

Her powerful performance with Big Brother and the Holding Company at the Monterey festival brought her to worldwide attention. As the money rolled in so did the drugs in greater quantities and the group folded at the end of 1968. Joplin quit drugs and booze as she played with new bands. But she chanced her arm once again while recording a new album and died having taken an unusually pure dose.

The coroner's report stated numerous needle marks - old and new - were present on her arms. The Rose, a 1979 movie starring Bette Midler, is based on Joplin's life.

Bass player with American 60s band The Association, **Brian Cole** died on February 8th 1972 from a heroin overdose. He was 27. His son Jordan would join The Association two decades later.

Beatles manager **Brian Samuel Epstein** died of a drugs overdose at his London home on August, 27th 1967. He was 32.

He had been depressed by his decreasing involvement with the Fab Four's affairs, his homosexuality and his drug dependency. Ironically, homosexuality would cease to be outlawed (and an imprisonable offence) by the end of 1967. Epstein, who trained as an actor in his teens, took The Beatles under his wing in 1961 after seeing them at The Cavern in Liverpool. He managed other popular 1960s acts (Gerry & The Pacemakers, Billy J. Kramer & The Dakotas, The Fourmost, and Cilla Black).

The major British record labels snubbed The Beatles but Epstein landed them a deal with Parlophone, a subsidiary of EMI.

He enjoyed their rise to super-stardom but remained a troubled soul in his personal life - haunted by a 1957 offence of importuning.

Friends, alerted by his housekeeper, broke into his bedroom and found him dead. The Beatles were in Bangor, Wales, for a meeting of the International Meditation Society.

Jimi Hendrix cancelled a concert scheduled for that night at the Saville Theatre (run by Epstein) as a mark of respect.

Jeremy Ward, sound engineer for The Mars Volta, was another 27-year-old to die from drug abuse in his Los Angeles home on May 25th 2003.

A band statement read: "We have collaborated with Jeremy for the past 10 years. He was the driving force of Defacto (their new album), and an integral part of The Mars Volta, who often went unnoticed because he chose to perform offstage.

"Jeremy will continue to be with us in spirit at every show and during the making of every record."

Grateful Dead founder member and keyboard player **Ron 'Pigpen' McKernan** died on March 8th 1973 from alcoholism. He was 27. Pigpen started drinking heavily in his rebellious teens and stayed firm with his trusty wine and Southern Comfort while his colleagues experimented with drugs.

As his health deteriorated, Keith Godchaux took over on keyboards though Pigpen would still appear with the band until his health gave him little choice in 1972. His epitaph on his grave reads:

'PIGPEN WAS AND IS NOW FOREVER ONE
OF THE GRATEFUL DEAD'.

Rudy Lewis, lead singer with The Drifters for four years, died from a drug overdose on May 20th 1964. He was 27.

He was found dead in his bed on May 21st – the morning when The Drifters were due to record Under The Boardwalk. Recording went ahead as scheduled with Johnny Moore assuming lead vocals.

Blues brothers **Bob 'The Bear' Hite** and **Al 'Blind Owl' Wilson** were the moving forces behind Canned Heat – formed in Los Angeles in 1965.

Both fell to drugs. Wilson died on the night of September 2nd/3rd 1970 in the garden of Hite's home, having camped out. He was depressed by his failing eyesight and is believed to have OD'd on heroin. He was 27. Hite tried to keep the group going. He died 11 years later (April 5th 1981) following a heart attack after collapsing at a gig at the Palomino Club in Los Angeles. He was 36.

David Byron died of a alcohol-induced heart attack at his Reading home on February 28th 1985. He was 38.

The Essex-born vocalist sang on ten albums by Uriah Heep – named after the character in the Charles Dickens novel David Copperfield. He was axed from the band in summer 1976 because of his heavy drinking.

He tried several projects with other musicians but never came to terms with his drink problem, collapsing on stage at London's Marquee club during one show towards the end of his life.

Uriah Heep bassist **Gary Thain** died of a heroin overdose on December 8th 1975. He was 26. After playing with bands in his native New Zealand, Thain moved to England to join New Nadir. He tried several projects after New Nadir split before getting a call to join Heep in the early 70s, replacing Mark Clarke midway through an American tour.

The first album he recorded with Heep was Demons & Wizards which became their most successful disc. Thain had started taking drugs as a teenager and his problems intensified throughout a busy 1973 with Heep. His scrawny body was being ravaged by drugs.

He was hospitalised for three weeks after receiving an electric shock on stage in Dallas, his wife Carol left him, he turned to heroin for the first time and Heep decided to fire him.

No bands would touch him because of his sickness, his second wife, Mika, left him and he needed another spell in hospital. His latest girlfriend, Yoko, found his body in the bathroom of his London flat.

Junkies have an affinity with bathrooms. The privacy helps them hide their habit. Bathrooms also have a habit of replacing deathbeds. Jim Morrison met his end in one, as did many others.

Malcolm Owen, singer with British punks The Ruts, died in his bath from a heroin overdose on July 14th 1980. He was 26. He was believed to have kicked his habit and then returned to heroin after his wife left him.

'Can I Use Your Bathroom?' was etched into the vinyl of the band's final single as a very deep black tribute to their frontman. The band continued for a while as The Ruts DC.

Jonathan Melvoin, keyboardist with Chicago band The Smashing Pumpkins, died from drugs in the shower of a New York hotel room on July 11th 1996. He was 34.

Melvoin and drummer Jimmy Chamberlin had been drinking and injecting

ROCK 'TIL YOU DROP

heroin at the Regency Hotel. Melvoin collapsed first, soon followed by his fellow junkie. When Chamberlin woke and couldn't rouse Melvoin, he called the band's security manager. They put Melvoin in a shower and achieving no results called the paramedics. Melvoin was already dead. Five days later Chamberlain was kicked out of the band. Melvoin's widow, Laura, sued the Pumpkins for failing to keep her husband off drugs. They made her a $10,000 settlement.

Candy Givens, singer with Colorado band Zephyr, drowned in a Jacuzzi after passing out from a mix of alcohol and drugs on January 30th 1984. She was 38. Candy and husband David had formed Zephyr – a rockin' band which helped launch future Deep Purple axeman Tommy Bolin.

After Zephyr split, Candy and David separated but performed together on and off with bands like the 4-Nikators. They met again in Boulder in 1984. Two weeks later she would be dead.

David Givens told an interviewer: "She had argued with her boyfriend after staying out late drinking with some of her less savoury friends. She had locked herself in the bathroom and started to run a tub for the Jacuzzi. She had taken two or three Mexican Quaaludes on top of her tequila high. She lost consciousness in the tub and drowned.

"Her boyfriend was in the next room the whole time, but by the time he got anxious and broke in, she was gone.

"I have the feeling that she was very surprised to find herself dead. She had always gotten away with tempting fate... until she died."

New York Dolls drummer **Bill Murcia** died in London on November 6th 1972. He was 21.

The Dolls were on tour in Britain with Rod Stewart And The Faces. Murcia passed out drunk after a show at London's Wembley Arena and drowned in a bath he'd been placed in to sober up.

James Honeyman-Scott, guitarist with The Pretenders, died on June 16th 1982 from a cocaine-induced heart attack. He was 25.

Ironically, two days earlier, bass player **Peter Farndon** had been kicked out of the band due to his drug abuses!

He died in a bathtub of a drug overdose on April 14th the following year. He was 30. At the time he was planning to launch a band with former Clash drummer Topper Headon,

Farndon and Honeyman-Scott both hailed from Hereford and moved to London where they met Ohio-born singer Chrissie Hynde and formed The Pretenders.

They got on the British New wave bandwagon and tasted chart success in 1979 with their cover of the Kinks song Stop Your Sobbing. Farndon and

Hynde became a couple until she fell for Kinks' star Ray Davies. She was pregnant with Davies's child when Farndon was sacked.

Two of the most famous British drummers suffered alcohol-related deaths.

Led Zeppelin drummer **John Henry Bonham** (aka Bonzo) choked on his own vomit at Jimmy Page's home in Windsor, London after a booze binge on September 25th 1980. He was 32.

His legendary drinking exploits earned him the nickname Heineken, but towards the end it had begun to affect his performances.

He was on medication to wean him off heroin, and on his final drinking session (as the band were rehearsing for an upcoming tour) he was alleged to have had 40 vodkas.

His death heralded the end of probably the greatest metal band.

The Who's manic drum destroyer **Keith Moon** died of a drug overdose in London on September 7th 1978. He was 32.

The Heminevrin tablets had been prescribed to help Moon kick his alcoholism. Moon died the day after attending a party, hosted by Paul and Linda McCartney, with his girl friend Annette Walter-Lax.

They were staying in Harry Nilsson's London flat at 12 Curzon Place – the same flat where Mama Cass had died a few years earlier.

Moon led a truly wild rock 'n roll life - his wife had left him when her paitience ran out. He and guitarist Pete Townshend were renowned for smashing up their equipment on stage. On an early American performance a broken piece from a cymbal lodged in Moon's leg. The band fought among themselves, wrecked hotel rooms (they were banned from the Holiday Inn group), drove cars into swimming pools – nothing was too outlandish.

The Who continued for many years, with Kenny Jones on the sticks, but would never rediscover the power of the early days with the Mooniac.

Fear Of God singer **Dawn Crosby** died on December 15th 1996 of liver failure brought on by years of excessive alcohol consumption. She was 33.

Fear Of God, a heavy metal Californian band, was formed in 1990 when Détente, one of Crosby's earlier bands, split.

Aussie rocker **Bon Scott** died after a booze binge on February 19th 1980. He was 33. The AC/DC singer choked on his own vomit in a car outside a friend's appartment in London. His family moved from Scotland to Fremantle, Australia when Ronald Belford Scott was six.

He played with The Spectors, The Valentines (who disbanded in 1970, a year after the group were arrested on drug charges) and then Fraternity.

He was forced to leave Fraternity in 1973. On returning to Australia from a European tour, Scott was involved in a motorbike accident that left him in a coma for three days and in hospital for several months. Scott began life in

AC/DC as their driver before landing the break that would turn him and them into rock legends. Singer Dave Evans failed to turn up for a show and Scott landed his job.

His performances, singing and writing provided the spark to make AC/DC one of the biggest hard-rock bands of their time.

London lad **Gary Holton**, frontman for 70s band Heavy Metal Kids and TV star in the comedy series Auf Wiedersehen Pet, died on October 25th 1985 of a heroin overdose. He was 35.

Holton, educated at Westminster School, worked in theatre with the Sadlers Wells Opera Company, the Old Vic Theatre Company and the Royal Shakespeare Company at Stratford. He toured with the musical Hair for two years before turning to rock and becoming a founder member of the HM Kids. The Kids had a whirlwind career before Holton returned to acting and landed roles in movies Quadrophenia and Breaking Glass plus several TV dramas.

His most famous role was as Wayne - the chirpy Cockney in Auf Wiedersehen Pet. Unlike his character, however, Holton was far from chirpy in private as the tabloid Press related tales of his heroin addiction and troubled love life.

He died at a friend's house in Wembley, London following a heavy drinking session. His girlfriend Janet McIllewan discovered him dead in bed.

He died bankrupt with action pending to recoup massive tax debts.

The coroner at his inquest recorded an open verdict. The post mortem had revealed alcohol, cannabis, morphine and valium in his blood.

"It must follow from the medical evidence that this man had a fix of heroin. The absence of any evidence to indicate when this was taken and the absence of evidence about finding a syringe and other material for drug abuse leaves enormous unanswered questions," stated the coroner.

Def Leppard guitarist **Steve Clark** died in his London home after taking a drink-drugs cocktail on January 8th 1991. He was 30.

Clark had been battling the booze for five years, was taking anti-depressants and painkillers after cracking three ribs in a fall. He was on sick leave from the band after it had become increasingly clear that he could not play his guitar because of the shakes.

A friend told the inquest that after returning to his Chelsea home from the pub the night before his death Clark downed a triple vodka, a quadruple vodka and a double brandy within 30 minutes. Clark passed out and his body was later discovered by his girlfriend.

Zac Foley, bass player with EMF, died on January 2nd 2002 after taking a cocktail of drink and drugs at a New Year party. He was 31. Born Zachary

ROCK 'TIL YOU DROP

Sebastian Rex James Foley, he helped found dance band EMF (Epsom Mad Funkers) in 1989 and the group were on the comeback trail with a US tour in the pipeline when he died.

The inquest heard that Foley was found dead at a friend's flat in Camden High Street after drinking beer and vodka and taking ecstasy, crack, morphine and barbiturates.

Christel Makaloy, who owned the flat, returned from work to discover Foley lying face down in her bedroom. Around him lay a crack pipe, a piece of burnt tin foil, a small amount of crack cocaine, an empty vodka bottle and cans of lager.

A local drugs official told the inquest that at one time Foley spent £400 a day for a period of two months on heroin alone.

EMF had a 1990 UK hit with Unbelievable which featured in the soundtrack to the film Coyote Ugly.

Country star **Keith Whitley** died on May 9th 1989 from alcoholism. He was 33. The Kentucky-born singer made his name with Ralph Stanley's Clinch Mountain Boys at the Grand Ole Opry.

He enjoyed a US Number One with When You Say Nothing At All the year before his death.

Country-rock great **Gram Parsons** died in The Joshua Tree Inn, California, from a drink-drug overdose shortly after midnight on September 19th 1973. He was 26.

He had been drinking tequila and Jack Daniels and taking heroin and morphine during the previous day. As his body was waiting to be flown to New Orleans for burial, his road manager Phil Kaufman and a friend, Michael Martin – both drunk – decided to perform their own cremation in accordance with Parsons's wishes.

They stole a hearse and then conned Los Angeles airport officials into handing over the coffin. They drove to the Joshua Tree desert, drenched the coffin and corpse with gasoline and enjoyed the bonfire. They were later charged with destroying the coffin and fined $700 - there was no law against stealing a corpse. The star's remaining remains were taken to New Orleans for the official burial.

Parsons, born Cecil Ingram Connor in Florida, recorded with The Byrds and The Flying Burrito Brothers, made highly-acclaimed solo projects (GP and Grievous Angel) and was inducted into the Rock And Roll Hall Of Fame.

Along the way he befriended members of the Rolling Stones. Close friends claimed his serious drug abuse startedwhen he spent time with them in France as they recorded Exile On Main Street.

ROCK 'TIL YOU DROP

Miss Christine, of the female 60s band GTO's, died on November 5th 1972 from an overdose of pain-killers in Cohasset, Massachusetts. She was 22. Born Christine Frka, she had been receiving treatment for a spinal problem. The GTO's were formed in Los Angeles under the wing of Frank Zappa. A meeting with Tiny Tim convinced the girls to ditch their surnames and become a band of Misses.

Miss Christine baby-sat for Zappa, dated Alice Cooper and hung around the rock-star set. She is the girl emerging from a tomb on the cover of Zappa's Hot Rats album.

The Flying Burrito Brothers recorded Christine's Tune about her. The title was changed to She's The Devil In Disguise after her death.

It gets her off to see a person crying
She's just the kind that you can do without
She's a devil in disguise
You can see it in her eyes
She's telling dirty lies
(Gram Parsons/Chris Hillman)

The GTO's recorded just one album, Permanent Damage, before disbanding after some members were busted for drug possession.

Jazz singer **Dinah Washington** (born Ruth Jones) died from a drug overdose after a drink binge on December 14th 1963. She was 39.

Born in Tuscaloosa, Alabama, Dinah loved singing and the fame and fortune it brought her – acquiring cars, clothes, jewellery and men. She had married for the seventh time when she died.

Jazz great **Bix Beiderbecke** died after a drinking binge in Queens, New York, on August 6th 1931. He was 28. One of the early white jazz men, Leon Bix Beiderbecke was a superb cornet player and composer.

He became an alcoholic – during the Prohibition era – and at one time in 1929 was sent to his parents' home in Iowa to recover from a nervous breakdown.

Charlie 'Bird' Parker died of drink and drug-related illnesses in New York on March 12th 1955. He was 34. One of the greatest bebop sax players of his generation, Parker suffered the excesses of alcohol and drugs (heroin). He developed ulcers and cirrhosis.

He was imprisoned in the psychiatric unit at Los Angeles jail after setting fire to his hotel room in 1946 and then spent six months in a rehab clinic.

His final performance – at Birdland, a New York club named after him – ended in a farce as he argued onstage with band members. He died eight days later in the suite of jazz patron Baroness Pannonica de Koenigswarter at the Stanhope on Fifth Avenue.

Baroness 'Nica' was well known in jazz circles. A member of the Rothschild family and a friend of Winston Churchill, she moved to the USA after the Second World War. Her homes would provide welcome refuge for many jazz musicians.

Average White Band drummer **Robbie McIntosh** died from a heroin overdose on September 23rd 1974. He was 24.

The band had completed a week's stint at the Los Angeles Troubadour Club and were chilling out at a party for Gregg Allman thrown at the home of millionaire Kenneth Moss.

McIntosh died from inhaling strychnine-based heroin which he thought was cocaine. Bandmate Alan Gorrie was saved by Allman's wife Cher who kept him awake. Steve Ferrone replaced McIntosh, becoming the first black member of the White Band.

G.G. Allin, whose proud claim to fame was as the vilest artist to emerge in the punk era, died from a cocaine/heroin overdose at a New York party on June 27th 1993. He was 36.

The Michigan madman (born Kevin Michael Allin) fronted such bands as the Murder Junkies & Toilet Rockers. His shows were torrents of abuse, performed sometimes in the nude. Razor blades and broken bottles were his props. The stage was his lavatory, too - the results being smeared, eaten or flung at the audience.

He would fight fans, have sex with some and mutilate himself while belting out ditties like Fucking The Dog (trust me, that is one of the tamer ones). Not surprisingly, his work received little airplay. Albums Freaks, Faggots, Drunks & Junkies, and America's Most Hated were cut on basic home recording equipment.

He assembled a hardcore cult following, and club managers continued to allow him to abuse their venues despite the fact that invariably riots would ensue. He had brushes with the law – totalling at least 50 – and was jailed for assaulting a girl fan. His defence was the groupie had asked him to chain and beat her.

He was released in 1993 and threatened to kill himself on stage. He was beaten to the punch by his drug overdose.

His funeral was as extreme as his life. Organised by his brother, GG's corpse was not treated to the customary tarting up by the funeral directors - he was laid to rest sporting a leather jacket and a jockstrap, clutching a mic in one hand and a bottle of Jack in the other.

Fans paid their due respect – playing with his privates, posing for photos and downing his Jack when the booze dried up at the wake.

Sex Pistols bassist **Sid Vicious** died from a heroin overdose in New York on February 2nd 1979. He was 21.

The British punk rocker had been partying at his new girlfriend's Greenwich Village apartment. They were celebrating his release on bail over charges that he had stabbed to death his previous girlfriend 'Nauseous Nancy' Spungen. The Pistols had broken up in January 1978 and Vicious and Spungen moved from London to New York.

Vicious (born John Simon Ritchie) was arrested at the famous Chelsea Hotel on October 12th after authorities had been alerted to a serious incident. Spungen (a dancer from Philadelphia) was dead. Police said there were signs of a struggle and a trail of blood leading from the disorderly bedroom to the bath of Room 100. Residents claimed Spungen often had bruises or a black eye.

Vicious was close to collapse as he denied murder at an opening court hearing. Pistols' mentor Malcom McLaren had flown in for the hearing and to try and get bail. Vicious was admitted to the hospital at Riker's Prison to undergo heroin detoxification.

His mum flew to see him, while back in London McLaren's boutique started selling T-shirts sporting an image of Vicious surrounded by a bunch of dead roses and the slogan She's Dead, I'm Alive, I'm Yours.

McLaren managed to persuade Virgin Records to stump up the $50,000 bail. Shortly after his release Vicious attempted suicide by consuming his whole supply of methadone (used to wean him off heroin) and slashing himself with a razor and a broken light bulb.

Vicious would soon be back at Riker's for attacking Patti Smith's brother Todd at Hurrah's disco in New York. He was there for seven weeks and was believed clean when he was released on bail again.

But he turned back to heroin at the release party - allegedly taking the fatal dose from his mother's purse.

He protested his innocence to the end, even though his mind (never in the best condition) was clearly befuddled. Some claim an irate drug dealer killed Spungen; others say it was a half-successful suicide pact.

Both Vicious and Spungen had said they expected to die young. Spungen: "I'll kill myself as soon as the first wrinkle appears."

Bob Stinson, guitarist with The Replacements until being kicked out because of his substance abuses, died in his Minneapolis appartment on February 18th 1995. He was 35.

Stinson was a zany performer, sporting garish stage clothing (even a nappy at one show) and sometimes appearing nude. He was forced out of

The Replacements in 1986, played in several Minneapolis bar bands before sliding completely downhill. His younger brother, Tommy, joined Guns 'N Roses as their bass player after The Replacements disbanded.

Brent Mydland died on July 26th 1990 at his home in Lafayette, near San Francisco, from a drug overdose. He was 37.

Mydland was the third Grateful Dead keyboard player to die. Ron (Pigpen) McKernan died in 1973, and Keith Godchaux in 1980.

The coroner's reported stated: "Lethal levels of morphine and cocaine in the blood ... the autopsy revealed a recent puncture mark of the left arm consistent with a recent intravenous injection prior to death."

The San Francisco Examiner reported that "Mydland's wife had left him recently, taking their two daughters with her...Mydland had experienced problems with alcohol in the past and was depressed about not having his family in his life."

Epic Soundtracks, British songwriter and drummer with several bands including Swell Maps and Crime & City Solution, was found dead in his London appartment on November 22nd 1997. He was 38.

Soundtracks, born Kevin Paul Godley, had been dead between one and two weeks, according to Tom Prendergast of Bar/None Records.

Friends had grown worried when Soundtracks didn't return calls. He had been taking anti-depressants after recently splitting with his girlfriend.

New Yorker **Tim Buckley**, one of the great band of 60s singer/songwriters, died from a drug overdose on June 29th 1975. He was 28.

As his career was taking off on the west coast, Buckley left his wife, Mary, after discovering she was pregnant. Mary gave birth to Jeff whose own musical career would be cut short by a tragic death.

Tim penned I Never Asked To Be Your Mountain for his ex-wife.

The 60s ended on a high for Buckley, but he soon began to suffer depression – believed to have been brought on by the poor reception for his album, Starsailor.

He bounced back to open the 1974 Knebworth festival – his first UK performance in six years. Recordings continued yet something was missing and Buckley expressed suicidal tendencies to friends.

After a show in Dallas he landed back in LA worse for wear and went to score some heroin. He was taken home where his second wife, Judy, tended to him as best she could before noticing he had turned blue. By the time the ambulance arrived Buckley was dead.

Singer/songwriter **Tim Hardin** died at his Hollywood home from a heroin overdose on December 29th 1980 – six days after his 39th birthday. His habit had started while serving with the Marines in the Far East. Bobby

Darin recorded Hardin's If I Were a Carpenter, enjoying much greater success than the composer.

He was an inconsistent live performer, and once fell asleep on stage at London's Royal Albert Hall. Hardin's drug abuse led to his wife, Susan, leaving their Woodstock home and moving with their son to LA. Hardin went to London for free treatment for his addiction. A cleaned up Hardin returned to the USA, got depressed and dirty again, accelerating his end.

West Arkeen, best known for co-writing a number of Guns 'N Roses songs, died of a drug overdose at his home in Los Angeles on May 30th 1997. He was 36.

Arkeen, who had just released an album with The Outpatience, had taken drugs to ease the pain from burns caused when his oven exploded.

Singer and bassist with San Francisco hardcore punk band Flipper, Will Shatter died of at home from a heroin overdose on December 9th 1987. He was 31.

The band reformed in 1990 with John Dougherty drafted in on bass. He was to die from heroin on Halloween 1997.

Parisian singer **Noel Rota** (aka Helno) died from a drug overdose at his parents' home on January 22nd 1993. He was 29.

Helno was lead singer with French New wave band Les Négresses Vertes – the name derived from an incident at a Paris club in 1987. The funsome five had dyed their hair green and were refused entry by a bouncer who branded them 'green niggers'.

They conquered the London dance scene in 1989 and became friendly with Madonna who championed their cause to international appeal. Their star shone brighter around the globe (rare for a French group) after a Christmas 1991 concert in Beirut (rare for any group).

The following year Helno began the rush downwards due to drink and drugs. Within 12 months he was dead and the remaining four band members would be too grief-stricken to record for two years.

New Yorker **Frankie Lymon**, lead vocalist with The Teenagers, died of a heroin overdose at his parents' home on February 27th 1968. He was 25.

Lymon was one of the early black teenage singing idols, recording songs like Why Do Fools Fall In Love?

After successful tours and radio/TV appearances in the USA, The Teenagers toured Britain in 1957 and released a second album called Frankie Lymon and The Teenagers at the London Palladium.

Lymon's career went downhill after he launched a solo career in 1958: his voice broke and his heroin addiction began. He tried rehab but lapsed and only escaped jail in 1966 by joining the army. The army soon kicked him out and hastened his descent. Bickering over rights to gain control of his material was confused when three women claimed to be his widow.

Frankie Lymon and The Teenagers were inducted into The Rock And Roll Hall of Fame in 1993.

Dwayne Goettel, keyboard player with New Wave band Skinny Puppy, died of a heroin overdose on August 23rd 1995 in his parents' home in Edmonton, Alberta. He was 31.

Frontman with Californian band Sublime, **Bradley James Nowell** died on May 25th 1996 from a heroin overdose. He was 28. The previous week he had married his fiancee Troy Dendekker. He had phoned her from his San Francisco hotel room on the day of his death to say how well the previous night's show had gone down in Petaluma.

When the band came to collect him, Nowell's beloved Dalmatian Lou guided them to his master's body. Nowell had been having treatment since 1992 to try and wean him off heroin, which he had started taking "to boost my creativity."

Chicago soul singer **Baby Huey** died from a drug-related heart attack on October 28th 1970. He was 26.

Huey, born James Ramsey, was an energetic and massive (400 pounds) frontman for Baby Huey & The Babysitters. The Babysitters played on for a while with teenager Chaka Khan (later of Rufus fame) as lead singer.

Founder member of Crazy Horse, **Danny Whitten** died of a heroin overdose on November 18th 1972. He was 29.

Crazy Horse shot to fame backing Neil Young, but Whitten was sacked shortly after the recording of their debut album because of his heroin addiction. The album features a classic ballad composed by Whitten – I Don't Want to Talk About It, which was later recorded by many others including Rod Stewart.

Young gave Whitten another chance as part of his backing band, but sacked him when he proved incapable of performing. Whitten died the very night of his dismissal.

Young would pay tribute to Whitten (and roadie Bruce Berry who also died from drugs) on his Tonight's The Night Album.

Vocalist with Californian punksters Germs, **Darby Crash** (born Jan Paul Breahm) died on December 7th 1980 from a heroin overdose. He was 21.

His brother had died from a heroin overdose while Jan was a child. The Germs made just one album, disbanded then reformed for a one-off gig in Los Angeles. Darby Crash died four days after that show.

Scrawled on a wall was: 'Here Lies Darby C...' leading some to deduce he committed suicide.

Hillel Slovak, founder guitarist with the Red Hot Chili Peppers, died of a heroin overdose on June 25th 1988. He was 26. Israeli-born Slovak is buried at Mount Sinai Memorial Park in Los Angeles.

The Chilis were born in LA where Slovak's family had moved when he was five. Slovak started doing drugs as the band was gradually establishing itself in the mid-80s. He died while the Chilis were working on Rockin' Freakapotamus, their fourth album.

Slovak's death hit the band hard and convinced singer Anthony Kiedis to kick his own habit. Drummer Jack Irons, who had known Slovak since their school days, suffered breakdowns which required hospital treatment.

New York Dolls guitarist **Johnny Thunders** was found dead from a drug overdose in a New Orleans hotel room on April 23rd 1991. He was 38.

Despite their short lifespan in the mid-70s, The Dolls gained a cult following and are regarded by many as the precursors of punk.

Thunders (born John Anthony Genzale) went on to form his own band The Heartbreakers. When his body was discovered it was bent double due to rigor mortis.

Los Angeles bluesman **Lester Butler** was killed by drug overdoses administered by two friends on May 10th 1998. He was 38.

The woman and her boyfriend were jailed for two-three years for involuntary manslaughter. Butler had passed out and they couldn't revive him in the bath so injected him with more cocaine on several occasions over the next 36 hours before seeking medical attention. Not surprisingly, Butler was pronounced dead on arrival at the LA clinic.

Stars such as Mick Jagger and Lenny Kravitz had performed with Butler and The Red Devils.

Guitarist **Mike Bloomfield** was found dead in his car of a drug overdose in San Francisco on February 15th 1981. He was 37.

Bloomfield learned his trade in his native Chicago in the 50s, jumping on stage as a teenager to jam with bluesmen in clubs where few white faces were seen.

He joined the Butterfield Blues Band in the 60s and performed with Bob Dylan at the famous 1965 Newport Folk Festival when Dylan shocked rock with his first live electric performance. He also starred on Dylan's epic Highway 61 Revisited album.

He left the Butterfield Blues Band in the mid-60s and headed west where he indulged in several solo and group projects with mixed results - due to poor health and drug abuse.

One of his last performances was as a guest at Dylan's gospel residency at San Francisco's Warfield Theatre in November 1980.

ROCK 'TIL YOU DROP

Paul Kossoff, guitar player with British band Free, died of a drug-related heart attack on March 19th 1976. He was 26.

Though he was at one time considered a possible replacement for Brian Jones in The Rolling Stones, Kossoff stayed with Free and enjoyed global lasting fame with their epic single All Right Now (1970).

Kossoff's drug problem and internal bickering prompted the band to fold in 1973. He almost died in a London clinic, then his heart finally packed in on a flight from Los Angeles to New York.

Guitarist **George Holton III** (aka Montague), of Atlanta band The Woggle, died from a drug overdose on May 13th 2003. He was 31.

Holton died in his sleep from an accidental overdose of medicine to treat his diabetes. A friend and fellow Atlanta musician **John Scott Rogers** had died two days earlier in a car accident.

Andrew Wood, singer with Seattle-based band Mother Love Bone, died on March 19th 1990 in hospital from a drug overdose. He was 24.

He had OD'd three days earlier but had been kept on a life-support machine at hospital. Pearl Jam emerged from the remnants of MLB.

Carl Crack, founder and singer of techno band Atari Teenage Riot, died in his Berlin flat on September 6th 2001 from drugs. He was 30. Crack (born Karl Bohm) had received treatment for mental problems. The post-mortem revealed pills and alcohol still in his system.

New York keyboard player **Michael Rudetski** was found dead from a drug overdose in London on August 6th 1987. He was 27.

He OD'd on heroin at the home of Culture Club singer Boy George, who had recently confessed his own drug addiction. Rudetski had played on the Culture Club album From Luxury To Heartache.

His parents unsuccessfully tried to sue Boy George.

Charlie Ondras, drummer with hardcore New York punk band Unsane, died of a heroin overdose in June 1992. He was 36. Unsane provoked outrage with the graphic violence and death depicted on their record sleeves.

Bass player with British band The Wonder Stuff, **Rob Jones** died on July 30th 1993 from a drug-related heart failure. He was 29.

He had left The Wonder Stuff a few years earlier and moved to New York where he and his wife Jessie formed The Bridge And Tunnel Crew.

Blind Melon frontman **Shannon Hoon** died of a drug overdose on the band's tour bus before a show in New Orleans on October 21st 1995. He was 28.

Hoon had long struggled with drug problems and had recently come out of rehab. He was forced to seek treatment at the insistence of band members after Hoon had had run-ins with the law for fighting and indecent exposure.

ROCK 'TIL YOU DROP

In 1996, the remaining members of Blind Melon compiled and released a collection of demos and outtakes. The album was named Nico in honor of Hoon's daughter, who was three months old when he died.

Guitarist with Seattle group 7 Year Bitch, **Stefanie Sargent** died from a heroin overdose on June 27th 1992. She was 24. Her death came just as 7 Year Bitch was about to release their debut album, Sick 'Em.

Lead guitarist with New York band Sha Na Na, **Vinnie Taylor** (born Chris Donald) died of a heroin overdose on April 17th 1974 in Charlottesville, Virginia. He was 25.

Sha Na Na (the name came from the 1950s hit Get A Job) were one of the star acts at the 1969 Woodstock Festival. The reformed band later appeared in the 1978 movie Grease.

Deep Purple guitarist **Tommy Bolin** died on December 4th 1976 from a drug overdose. He was 25.

Bolin had passed out the previous night at his Miami hotel following a binge and roadies had put him to bed.

The following morning, his girlfriend called an ambulance but Bolin died before it arrived. Cause of death was reported as multiple drug intoxication.

The Sioux City guitarist – self-taught – played with Zephyr and The James Gang before being handed the awesome task of replacing Ritchie Blackmore in Deep Purple.

Blackmore – founder member of the legendary British rock band – had decided to go solo in April 1975. On singer David Coverdale's recommendation, Bolin passed an audition in California.

They recorded an album later that year, Come Taste The Band, before going on the road in Australia, Japan and the USA.

The band became aware of Bolin's heroin addiction while in the Far East. The end soon came after an unsuccessful tour of Britain where fans clamoured for Blackmore. Purple disbanded that summer.

Bolin returned to the States to record and tour with The Tommy Bolin Band. He died the day after a show in Miami where his band was support act to the Jeff Beck group.

Rolling Stone magazine reported: "He was buried December 10th in the family plot in Calvary Cemetery in Sioux City.

"Karen (his ex-girlfriend Karen Ulibarri) flew from England to attend along with 350 other people. She put a ring on his finger that Jimi Hendrix had been wearing the day he died (a gift to Bolin from Deep Purple's manager). Karen had been saving it for Tommy because he kept losing it."

Houston hip-hop producer **DJ Screw** died on November 16th 2000 after taking a cocktail of drink and drugs. He was 30. DJ Screw (born Robert

Earl Davis junior) was found in the bathroom of his studio.

Peter Rosen, bass player with Eric Burdon's War, died in 1969 from a drug overdose. He was 25.

Rob Graves (aka Rob Ritter), bass player with several gothic groups most notably LA-based Thelonius Monster and 45 Grave, died of a heroin overdose on June 28th 1990. He was 30.

Gregory Herbert, a lauded jazz sax player, died of a cocaine overdose on January 31st 1978 in Amsterdam while touring with legendary American band Blood, Sweat and Tears. He was 30.

Jon-Jon Paulos, drummer with Chicago band The Buckinghams, died on March 26th 1980 from a heart attack brought on by drug abuse. He was 32.

Nigel Preston, drummer with British gothic bands Cult, Theatre of Hate and The Sex Gang Children, died from an overdose on May 7th 1992. He was 33.

Stacy Guess, trumpeter and guitarist, died from a heroin overdose on March 11th 1998. He was 33. His drug addiction had forced him out of his biggest band, the North Carolina-based Squirrel Nut Zippers.

Drummer **Wells Kelly** died of an overdose while on tour with Meat Loaf in England on October 29th 1984. He was 35. He had previously played with New York band Orleans.

Ken Montgomery (aka Dimwit) died on September 27th 1994 from a heroin overdose. He was 36.

Dimwit played drums with Canadian punk band D. O. A. among others.

MEDICAL

ACCESS to the best physicians, psychiatrists, fitness trainers and lifestyle gurus can often amount to little – even for the greats of rock.

Bob Marley visited the world's leading specialists yet could not whip the cancer that gripped his proud body.

And what good would an expert dietician be to someone who insisted on eating until he couldn't tie his shoelaces?

New organs, surgery and medication can stave off the inevitable for only so long. Heart disease and cancer are by far the two biggest killers in the USA, causing more than half the fatalities there. It is a similar situation in the UK where someone suffers a heart attack every two minutes (2003 British Heart Foundation statistics).

Lack of exercise, increased drinking and poor diet leading to weight problems are the main cause of heart ailments.

Gigantic hip-hopper **Christopher Rios** (aka Big Pun or Big Punisher) died from a heart attack on Monday, February 7th 2000. He was 28 years old and weighed 698 pounds.

One friend reported that Big Pun ate "until he couldn't tie his shoelaces." Doctors believe his sudden death was caused by a long-standing heart condition that resulted from his extreme obesity. His heart was three times the normal size.

He collapsed at the Crowne Plaza Hotel in White Plains, New York, where he and his family were staying while their house was being renovated. His wife Liza called Rios's friend, Fat Joe, alarmed that Rios had stopped breathing.

"I assumed the worst, when somebody says he stopped breathing and don't have a pulse," said Fat Joe. "But it was like slow motion. I went over there and saw the paramedics working on him and they just covered him up. He was still breathing until he got to the hospital and they was working really hard on him, trying to revive him.

"He was so big and he knew his weight was causing a health problem. For a long time, even though he was a big guy, he could do whatever he wanted. He'd play sports with us and everything. But as time went on, his health got worse."

Rios had entered a diet program at Duke University the previous summer and lost some weight. But Joe says that Rios quickly gained the weight back. "I'm heavy myself and it's like, I know that losing weight is a real fight."

Darren 'The Human Beat Box' Robinson died from a heart attack in Rosedale, New York, on December 10th 1995. He was 28.

He acquired his nickname due to his ability to 'beatbox': make percussion sounds with his mouth. He was a member of The Disco Three, who changed their name to Fat Boys after their manager was stung by a $350 bill for "extra breakfasts" during a European tour in 1983. Robinson weighed in at around 450 pounds when he died.

The larger than life **Mama Cass Elliott** (238lb) died of a heart attack brought on by obesity on July 29th 1974. She was 32.

Initial reports claiming she died by choking on a ham sandwich were disproved by the post mortem.

Cass (born Ellen Naomi Cohen) had a huge hit with California Dreamin' with the Mamas and the Papas before launching a successful solo career when the group split in 1971.

She had a long battle with her weight – being twice the average for her build – and died in a London flat owned by Harry Nilsson after performing two sold-out shows at the Palladium.

Who drummer Keith Moon would die at the same flat a few years later.

Powerful Detroit vocalist **Florence Ballard** died on February 22nd 1976 from a sudden heart failure provoked by medication for high blood pressure and weight loss. She was 32.

Ballard's music career began as a 14-year-old under the wing of Milton Jenkins – manager of The Primes, an early incarnation of The Temptations.

The Primettes were born and developed into The Supremes. Summer 1964 saw The Supremes top the US charts with Where Did Our Love Go – the first of five No. 1s in a year. They were suddenly Motown's hottest act.

Florence was jealous of Diana Ross assuming the role of group leader and began drinking heavily and putting on weight. She left the group in 1967, and the group was renamed Diana Ross and the Supremes.

Her solo career never took off in the big league; she needed welfare support to raise her three children after splitting from husband Tommy Chapman.

She had reconciled with Chapman and her career seemed set for a new phase when she was rushed to hospital and died from a blood clot in an artery. Diana Ross was jeered at Flo's Detroit funeral, which was conducted by Reverend C. L. Franklin (Aretha's father) and attended by the greats of Motown plus thousands of fans.

Karen Carpenter died on February 4th 1983 of heart failure caused by anorexia nervosa. She was 32.

The vocalist/drummer had started starving herself eight years previously, taking pills, inducing vomit and drinking water and eating little if anything, after a review commented on her chubbiness. She had sought psychiatric help to no avail. At one point Karen weighed just 80lb but had managed to increase to 110lb – almost the normal weight for a woman 5ft 4in tall.

The Grammy-winning Carpenters (Karen and brother Richard) hailed from New Haven, Connecticut but grew up in California. They were the best-selling group in America in the 1970s with eight gold and five platinum albums and many hit singles such as Close To You and We've Only Just Begun.

Karen collapsed in a wardrobe closet at her parent's home in Downey, California and died later in hospital.

Two years after her death The Washington Post reported that she died from "cardio toxicity brought on by the chemical emetine. Experts now agree she had misused a common, over-the-counter drug called ipecac.

"A foul-smelling, amber-coloured drug, syrup of ipecac has been sold in drugstores for years to induce vomiting in poison victims. General practitioners have long recommended having a bottle in the medicine chest as a cheap antidote; a one-ounce bottle costs only about $2.

"But the fact is that ipecac, in large dose, may cause irreversible damage to the heart, and if taken repeatedly, is a lethal poison."

Music, movies and TV star **Bobby Darin** (born Walden Robert Cassotto) died on December 20th 1973 from heart problems exacerbated by a trip to the dentist. He was 37.

His dental visit left him with septicaemia. By the time it was discovered, Darin was in a coma and his heart valves which had been replaced in 1971 required more surgical attention. He was not able to survive the surgery.

Darin, who had had heart problems since his childhood, scored a number one hit with Mack The Knife (nine weeks in 1959). He featured in several movies, was nominated for an Oscar and had his own TV series in the early 70s. He was active in politics and campaigned for the assassinated Senator Robert Kennedy.

Darin had no funeral, preferring to donate his body to UCLA Medical Centre. No grave marks his passing. He was inducted into the Rock And Roll Hall of Fame in 1990.

Composer/producer **Bert Berns** died following a heart attack in his hotel room on December 30th 1967 in his native New York. He was 38. He had lived with a weak heart since suffering a serious fever in his childhood.

Berns (and co-writer Phil Medley) wrote The Beatles' smash-hit Twist And Shout. Berns also penned classics like Under The Boardwalk (Drifters), Brown-Eyed Girl (Van Morrison/Them) and Everybody Needs Somebody To Love (Rolling Stones/Solomon Burke).

Bee Gees' sibling **Andy Gibb** died in Oxford on March 10th 1988 from myocarditis - a heart disease. He was 30.

Gibb, who had Number One hits with I Just Want To Be Your Everything and (Love Is) Thicker Than Water, had been admitted to the John Radcliffe Hospital three days earlier after complaining of stomach pains.

Ilari 'CLAUDE' Peltola, singer with Finnish metal rockers Smack, died from heart failure on September 22nd 1996. He was 30. Though they struggled to make much of an impact outside Scandinavia, Smack can count Nirvana and Guns 'N Roses among their fan club.

Founder member and lead vocalist with The Drifters, **Clyde Lensley McPhatter** died from a heart attack on June 13th 1972. He was 39.

His career with The Drifters was cut short when he was drafted into the American forces in 1955 but he later enjoyed some success as a solo artist and was inducted into Rock And Roll Hall Of Fame in 1987 – a year before The Drifters.

Dave Williams, lead singer of Drowning Pool, was found dead on the band's tour bus in Manassas, Virginia on August 14th 2002. He was 30.

The Dallas quartet was on tour with Ozzfest and had played in Noblesville, Indiana, the previous day. Williams died from cardiomyopathy, a disease of the heart muscle. He had never been diagnosed as having the illness.

Californian **Jeff Porcaro**, a top session drummer and member of Toto, died following a heart attack on August 5th 1992. He was 38.

Porcaro's post mortem revealed he suffered from an undiagnosed cardiac problem and the fatal attack was believed to have been sparked by a garden weed killer and not cocaine, as some alleged.

Porcaro counted a multitude of star names among his clients: Barbra Streisand, Sonny And Cher, Steely Dan and Michael Jackson.

Family and friends established The Jeff Porcaro Memorial Fund to provide music scholarships to LA students.

Jimmy McCulloch, Glasgow-born guitarist with Paul McCartney's Wings and many others, died in London on September 27th 1979 following a heart attack brought on by drug abuse. He was 26.

McCulloch had been playing in bands since he was 13. He performed with his older brother Jack (drums) in The Jaygars (later named One In A Million). He formed Thunderclap Newman in 1969 and that summer the band enjoyed a No.1 UK hit with Something In The Air.

London-born **John Glascock**, bass player with Chicken Shack and Jethro Tull, died from a long-standing heart illness on November 17th 1979. He was 28. A tooth infection caused weakening of a heart valve. He was forced to abandon a Tull tour and eventually had to leave the band. Despite surgery, he never recovered.

Hollywood-born slide guitar supreme **Lowell George** died from a heart attack in Arlington, Virginia on June 29th, 1979. He was 34.

After playing with Frank Zappa's Mothers Of Invention, George left to form Little Feat who made some classic rock songs including Willin' and Dixie Chicken. George suffered with his health and weight and left Little Feat in 1978. He passed away the day after performing a solo concert at George Washington University, Washington DC.

His ashes were scattered on the Pacific Ocean.

Patrick Waite, a founder member of Birmingham band Musical Youth, died of a rare heart disease on February 18th 1993. He was 24.

Musical Youth had a Number 1 hit with Pass The Dutchie (in praise of marijuana) in 1982. Patrick's drug problems led to the teenagers splitting up in the mid-80s and he turned to a life of petty crime.

He was convicted and served time in jail for various offences: reckless driving, fraud, assaulting police and robbing a pregnant woman at knifepoint. He was awaiting trial for drug possession when he collapsed and died.

London-born guitarist **Snakefinger** (born Philip Lithman) died of a heart attack in his sleep while on tour with The Vestal Virgins in Linz, Austria on July 1st, 1987. He was 38.

Snakefinger had never fully recovered from a coronary thrombosis he suffered in Melbourne in 1981. After performing in Chilli Willi and Red Hot Peppers, Lithman hooked up with Californian band The Residents who nicknamed him Snakefinger due to his nimble-fingered dexterity.

Hank Williams died of a heart attack on New Year's Day 1953. He was 29. The country legend (born Hiram Williams), who composed hits such as Your Cheatin' Heart and I'm So Lonesome I Could Cry, was a rebel in permanent turmoil. He trashed hotel rooms before Keith Moon started school.

He drank, gambled and took drugs (some admittedly for a painful back problem). He often failed to turn up for concerts; when he did he was often too drunk to perform. The Grand Ole Opry booted him out and warned him not to return until he had sobered up.

He was heading for a show in Canton, Ohio when he died. Flights had been cancelled due to bad weather so he hired a 17-year-old student, Charles Carr, to drive his Cadillac.

Carr told his story to an Alabama newspaper 50 years after Williams's death. He believes Williams died somewhere between Bristol, Tennessee and Oak Hill, West Virginia.

Williams was wearing white cowboy boots, a stylish blue overcoat and a white fedora when he left Knoxville at 10.45pm on New Year's Eve en route to a concert 500 snowy miles north.

He became increasingly concerned about the eerie silence in the back seat. He pulled off the road to check on Williams. Carr said: "I reached back to put the blanket back over him and I felt a little unnatural resistance from his arm."

Carr pulled into the next service station and was informed the nearest hospital was at Oak Hill, six miles away. "I ran in and explained my situation to the two interns who were in the hospital," said Carr. "They came out and looked at Hank and said, 'He's dead.'

"I asked 'em, 'Can't you do something to revive him?' One of them looked at me and said, 'No, he's just dead.'"

Thin Lizzy frontman **Phil Lynott** died on January 4th 1986 from heart failure brought on by drug abuse. He was 34.

He had collapsed the previous Christmas Day at his Richmond, London home. Lynott was raised by his Irish mother in Dublin and Manchester after his Brazilian father left them when he was just three weeks old.

Thin Lizzy (named after cartoon character Tin Lizzie) was born in 1969 and after a quiet start they hit the big time in 1973 with Whiskey In The Jar – a rock classic based on an Irish folk song and originally slated as a B side!

They also enjoyed success Stateside with hits like The Boys Are Back In Town and several big-selling albums despite many changes of musicians.

But Lynott's hard-living sex-n-drugs-n-rock-n-roll lifestyle took its gradual toll. Not even hepatitis (which forced him to curtail a USA tour) could persuade him to change his ways.

Lynott said: "The doctor told me to give up drugs, sex and alcohol...No way! So I gave up half of them. I won't tell you which half. The illness made me very sensible."

Thin Lizzy called it a day in 1983 after playing at the Reading Festival.

Pianist with the Patti Smith Group, **Richard Sohl** died from a heart attack on June 3rd 1990. He was 37. He was nicknamed DNV as he resembled the young boy in the movie Death In Venice.

Country singer/songwriter **Tom Jans** died from a heart attack (some say drug-related) at his Santa Monica home on March, 25th 1984. He was 35.

He was in a motor accident shortly before his death. He worked with American stars such as Joan Baez (and her sister Mimi Farina), Tom Waits and Bette Midler.

Van (The Hustle) McCoy died of a heart attack at Englewood, New Jersey on July 6th 1979. He was 39.

McCoy's true love was composing and he wrote for leading lights like Aretha Franklin, Gladys Knight, Roberta Flack, Jackie Wilson and Tom Jones. But it was his hit album Disco Baby (featuring Grammy winner The Hustle) which propelled him into global fame.

Aids emerged as the scary, shock illness in the 1980s, clouded initially by much misinformation on exactly how one could contract it.

Jobriath was one of the early musician victims. He also claimed to be the first openly gay rock star. Born Bruce Wayne Campbell, Jobriath died of Aids at his home in New York's Chelsea Hotel in July 1983. He was 37.

He had been in the original stage cast of the musical Hair. Manager/promoter Jerry Brandt resurrected Jobriath's career as the artist was heading downhill fast on drink, drugs and sexcess.

Peter Frampton and Led Zeppelin bassist John Paul Jones feature on Jobriath's self-titled debut album released in October 1973. Jobriath confirmed his homosexuality to an eager Press at the album's launch.

Jobriath was promoted as the 'True Fairy Of Rock 'n' Roll' – a dig at David Bowie who enjoyed massive success at the time.

The fall came speedily: Brandt and their label, Elektra, dropped Jobriath. His music career ended and he tried to break into movies before dying in 1983 – he had been dead for some time before his body was discovered.

Klaus Nomi (born Klaus Sperber) died from Aids on August 6th 1983. He was 38. A German who moved to New York, Nomi possessed an incredible vocal range from soprano to baritone. Equally extraordinary was his appearance. He was one of the early New Romantics, sporting make-up and extravagant garb on and off stage.

He got his break as back-up singer for David Bowie on Saturday Night Live and went on to perform theatrical avant-garde stage shows of his own. Mon Coeur from the Saint-Saens opera Samson and Delilah often closed his shows.

London-born Level 42 guitarist **Alan Murphy**, who also played with Go West, Scritti Politti, Kate Bush and Mike & The Mechanics, died of AIDS-related pneumonia on October 19th, 1989. He was 35.

One of his last recordings was Rocket Man with Kate Bush. The video, released after his death in 1990, features a guitar lying on a chair.

Billy Lyall, the former Bay City Roller and Pilot star, died in December

1989 from an Aids-related illness. He was 36. Lyall (keyboards/vocals) was in the original Rollers - before they developed into tartan-clad teeny-boppers. Pilot enjoyed a spell in the limelight from 1974-77 and scored a Number One UK hit with January - fittingly in January 1975.

Black Sabbath singer **Ray Gillen** (post Ozzy Osbourne) died from Aids at his New Jersey home on December 3rd 1993. He was 33.

Gillen had replaced Glenn Hughes as Sabbath vocalist in 1986. Hughes organised a memorial gig for Gillen the year after his death.

Guitarist with Athens, Georgia band The B-52's, **Ricky Wilson** died from Aids-related pneumonia on October 13th 1985. He was 32.

Ricky's sister Cindy was vocalist with the band which was named after the 1950s-style hair-do she sported. Ricky was so ashamed of contracting Aids that he never informed his sister.

Many outside the world of reggae mourned when the great **Bob Marley** died of cancer on May 11th 1981. He was 36.

Robert Nesta Marley was born in February 1945 to Captain Norval Marley, a 50-year-old white British serviceman, and his recent wife of just 18, Cedella, in his grandfather's house high in the Jamaican mountains at Nine Mile High.

His father soon left and mother and son moved to the Kingston suburb of Trenchtown. Bob fell deeper in love with music and there met friends who would soon become The Wailers.

The band developed a following in Jamaica but their big break came fortuitously when they were broke!

The Wailers were stranded in London with no funds to fly home. Marley went to see Island Records chief Chris Blackwell who signed them to his label. The £8,000 was money well spent by Blackwell. They flew home to Jamaica, recorded Catch A Fire and embarked on a crusade to take reggae around the world.

They gathered an international following by supporting acts such as Bruce Springsteen and Sly And The Family Stone in the USA.

The Wailers had a smash with No Woman, No Cry; Eric Clapton recorded Marley's I Shot The Sheriff; and Rolling Stone named them band of the year in 1976.

Great albums followed: Rastaman Vibration and Exodus. It was on the 1977 European tour that Marley first became ill. His toenail was ripped off in a football game in Paris but the wound did not heal properly.

Worried crew members persuaded him to seek medical help, and he saw specialists in London who discovered cancer and recommended amputation. That was against Marley's Rastafarian convictions but he did allow a

Miami surgeon to perform a skin graft on his right toe. Marley had a disturbing seizure in New York's Central Park while out jogging in September 1980. The previous night he had been close to collapse on stage at Madison Square Garden.

Despite his health scares, Marley pressed on with the tour to Pittsburgh for what would turn out to be his final live performance on September 23rd at the Stanley Theater.

Cancer was discovered in his brain, liver and lungs and was spreading. He had treatment in New York and then went to Germany to be treated by specialist Dr. Josef Issels. After several weeks of treatment Dr Issels informed Marley that he could do no more to help him. He flew to Miami and died two days later.

He was buried in mausoleum at Nine Mile High – the village of his birth. After his death he was awarded Jamaica's Order of Merit.

Brian 'Too Loud' MacLeod, award-winning producer and guitarist with Canadian bands Chilliwack and Headpins, died on April 25th 1992 from lung cancer. He was 39. Headpins' classic 1982 debut album TURN IT LOUD went double platinum (two million sales).

Harold McNair, a saxophonist and flautist from Jamaica, died in London from cancer on March 26th 1971. He was 39.

He played on the soundtrack for the film Kes and performed with artists such as Donovan, Ginger Baker and John Martyn.

"He was a very sweet little guy, very unassuming, very beautiful, very good flute player and a great alto player. He was definitely the best flute player I've ever heard. Nobody swung like him. They called him Little Jesus," Martyn told ZigZag magazine.

Jamaican producer, composer and singer **Keith Hudson** died from lung cancer in 1984. He was 37. He was at the forefront of the DJ explosion in the 1970s.

Melanie Susan Appleby, one half of the London duo Mel & Kim, died from spinal cancer exacerbated by pneumonia on January 18th 1990. She was 23. The sisters provided song-writing team Stock, Aitken & Waterman with their first number one single – Respectable – in 1987.

Mike Patto, who played guitar and sang with many groups in the 60s and 70s including Patto, Spooky Tooth and Boxer, died on March 4th 1979 after a long struggle against throat cancer. He was 36.

He was born Michael McCarthy but assumed his stage name after playing with a guitarist called Johnny Patto at a Butlin's Holiday Camp.

Stunning American singer **Minnie Riperton** died of breast cancer on July 12th 1979. She was 31. Minnie began recording as a teenager at the famous

Chess Studios in Chicago in the early 60s. She shot to worldwide fame with her 1974 album Perfect Angel. Stevie Wonder helped on the production of the album which featured the smash hit single Lovin' You .

Minnie surprised a national TV audience in 1976 by revealing on the Johnny Carson Show that she had breast cancer and had had surgery.

This began a personal crusade to increase breast cancer awareness in the USA, performing at many charity events. President Jimmy Carter presented Minnie with the American Cancer Society's 'Courage Award' in 1977.

Lead singer with Ronnie and the Hi-Lites, **Ronnie Goodson** died on November 4th 1980 from brain cancer. He was 33. The New Jersey band was originally called the Cascades but were renamed after Ronnie joined them.

Motown star **Tammi Terrell** (born Thomasina Montgomery in Philadelphia) died on March 16th 1970 of brain cancer. She was 24.

The cancer was diagnosed after she collapsed onstage while singing with Marvin Gaye in 1967 at Hampden-Sydney College, near Norfolk, Virginia. They recorded an album which included the classic Ain't No Mountain High Enough.

The cancer is believed to have started due to the physical abuse Tammi had suffered at the hands of boyfriends. She had eight operations to try to cure her.

O'Jays singer **William Powell** died on May 26th 1977 from cancer in his hometown of Canton, Ohio. He was 35.

The band, five school pals, recorded their first single Miracles as The Mascots. A local DJ called Eddie O'Jay played the single so often that the boys changed their name out of gratitude. Early 70s songs Back Stabbers and Love Train were hits on both sides of the Atlantic.

Memphis-born **Bill Black** (born William Patton Black) was the bassist of the Scotty & Bill duo that backed Elvis Presley on his earliest live performances. He died from a brain tumour on October 21st 1965, aged 39.

Scotty & Bill backed Elvis from 1954-57 before leaving after a pay dispute. He formed the Bill Black Combo which had some US chart success and continued touring for many years after his death.

Mississippi bluesman **Junior Parker** (born Herman Parker Jr.) died in Chicago on November 18th 1971 from a brain tumour. He was 39.

Ike Turner gave Little Junior Parker his break into recording with Modern Records in 1952. Parker later recorded for Sun Records.

He was inducted into the Blues Hall Of Fame in 2001.

Mary-Ann Ganser of the Shangri-Las, an early bad girl group, died from encephalitis in 1970. She was 22. The band, comprising identical twins

Marge and Mary-Ann Ganser and sisters Betty and Mary Weiss, came out of Queens, New York, in the early 1960s and had several smash hits, most notably Leader Of The Pack, before splitting in 1967.

Seattle jazz singer **Mary Lofstrom** died from ovarian cancer and scleroderma, a rare rheumatic disease, on October 20th 2003. She was 38.

Lofstrom, who promoted lesbianism through her lyrics, earned a 2003 Outmusic Award for Outstanding New Recording Female for Ginger Comes to Stay.

Nigerian percussionist **Reebop Kwaku Baah** died of a brain haemorrhage after collapsing on stage in Stockholm on January 12th 1982. He was 38.

Baah played with Traffic, Can and Ginger Baker's Airforce and worked with many top stars including The Rolling Stones and Eric Clapton.

Sandy Denny, singer with British folk band Fairport Convention, died of a brain haemorrhage on April 21st 1978. She was 31. She had been in a coma for a week after falling down steps at a friend's house.

Sandy had two spells with Fairport, and also recorded with her own band, Fotheringay, and as a solo artist. Robert Plant's favourite female vocalist, sings backing vocals on The Battle Of Evermore on Led Zeppelin IV.

Original member of The Beatles, **Stu Sutcliff** died of a brain haemorrhage on April 10th 1962. He was 21.

Sutcliff (bass/vocals) had been invited to join the band in January 1960 by John Lennon, a fellow art student. He lasted less than 12 months before quitting to become an artist.

He had begun complaining of headaches during their Hamburg shows and passed away just as the Fab Four were about to hit the big time.

Detroit bass man **Terome 'T-bone' Hannon** died of a brain aneurysm on September 4th 2003. He was 39. He had been due to go on the road two weeks later with Jewel, who cancelled her North American tour. Hannon backed many artists, including Shania Twain.

Chuck Schuldiner, singer and guitarist with death metal band Death, died of a brain tumour on December 13th 2001. He was 34.

Jeffrey Lee Pierce, singer and founder of Los Angeles band The Gun Club, died of a brain haemorrhage on March 31st 1996. He was 37.

Pierce, who had battled for years against alcohol and drug abuse, was visiting his father when he suffered his fatal stroke.

The multi-talented **Chris Wood** died in his native Birmingham on July 12th 1983 from pneumonia brought on by drink and drug problem. He was 39. Wood was a founder member of Traffic, starring on sax, flute, organ and vocals. He also played with Ginger Baker's Airforce.

He also appears on Jimi Hendrix's Electric Ladyland album recorded in

New York. He married singer Jeanette Jacobs (Dr. John's band) and, though they had divorced, his health deteriorated after her death from a fit in 1982. Wood had started drinking heavily to conquer his fear of flying.

Atlanta-born blues singer and composer **Harold 'Chuck' Willis** died from stomach ulcers on April 10th 1958. He was 30. Songs such as I Feel So Bad and It's Too Late were covered by the likes of Elvis and Otis Redding.

One of the leading lights in the 1950s-60s British blues circles, **Cyril Davies** died on January 7th 1964 from leukaemia. He was 31.

His band Blues Incorporated initially featured drummer Charlie Watts (Rolling Stones) and bassist Jack Bruce (Cream). He is credited with teaching Stones duo Mick Jagger and Brian Jones to play harmonica.

Guitar giants Jimmy Page and Jeff Beck were others to sit in with Davies during the London music explosion of the early 60s.

The original lead singer/song-writer with American soul band Main Ingredient, **Don McPherson** died on July 4th 1971 from leukaemia. He was 29. McPherson was replaced as lead vocalist by Cuba Gooding – father of movie star Cuba Gooding Jr.

Father Of Country Music **Jimmie Rodgers** died on May 26th 1933 from tuberculosis. He was 32. Rodgers worked on railroads – hence his tag The Singing Brakeman – until his illness forced him to quit.

He came to the attention of Ralph Peer – a talent-spotter in the south for the Victor label. Rodgers went on to record and have massive hits with his unique blue-yodelling until his early death.

He was a founder member of the Rock And Roll Hall Of Fame. Bob Dylan assembled a star-studded line-up (Bono, Mellencamp, Van Morrison and others) to record The Songs of Jimmie Rodgers: A Tribute in 1997.

Rock and roller **Gene Vincent** (born Vincent Eugene Craddock) died in Los Angeles on October 12th 1971 from abdominal illness brought on by heavy drinking and ulcers. He was 36.

Be-Bop-A-Lula – based on a cartoon character Little Lulu – was the Virginian's biggest hit. He enjoyed greater popularity in Britain than back home and moved there in 1959. The following year he was injured in the motor accident which claimed Eddie Cochran's life.

Londoner **Matthew Ashman**, guitarist with New Wave bands Adam & the Ants and Bow Wow Wow, died on November 21st 1995 in London from diabetes He was 35.

Michael Ferguson, keyboard player with San Francisco hippies The Charlatans and creator of the first acid art rock poster, went blind from diabetes before dying of the disease in 1979. He was 34.

His innovative poster promoted The Charlatans' concert at the Red Dog

Saloon in Nevada in 1965 and sparked a new trend in concert posters.

American blues and country guitarist, **Peter Laughner** died on June 22nd 1977 from pancreatis brought on by drink and drug abuse. He was 24.

He featured in many bands, including Pere Ubu. He died in his sleep after making a home recording on a cassette tape.

Singer with New York punk band Surgery, **Sean McDonnell** died on January 18th 1995 in a Brooklyn hospital after suffering an asthma attack. He was 29.

Guitar player with Chicago R&B group The Sheppards, **Kermit Chandler** died on February 22nd 1981 after a long illness. He was 37.

Lefty Baker (born Eustace Britchforth), who played with Chicago 60s band Spanky And Our Gang, died on August 11th 1971. He was 29. Spanky's **Malcolm Hale** died of cirrhosis on October 31st 1968. He was 37.

Chicago singer/song-writer **Steve Goodman** died of leukaemia on September 20th 1984. He was 36.

His first Grammy award came shortly after his death – Willie Nelson had a Number One hit with Goodman's City of New Orleans and it landed the Grammy for Best Country Song. Unfinished Business – an album released after his death – won a Grammy in 1986.

Ty Brian, guitar player with Mersey band Rory Storm & the Hurricanes, died in 1967 in hospital from complications following an appendectomy. He was 26.

Jazz guitarist **Eddie Lang** died on March 26th 1933 in a New York hospital after suffering massive blood loss during tonsil surgery. He was 29.

Lang was much in demand for recordings and concerts. He regularly backed Bing Crosby who became a good friend. Crosby was devastated by Lang's death as he had urged him to undergo surgery to cure his laryngitis.

Jazz drummer **Chick Webb** (born William Henry Webb) died after surgery in his native Baltimore on June 16th 1939. He was 30.

He contracted spinal tuberculosis while just three years old. The disease left Chick with a hunchback and little use of his legs. Doctors suggested drumming to ease his joints. He became one of the top bandleaders, using a custom-made kit to pound away.

Joseph Calleja (aka Joe C) died in his sleep at his home in Taylor, Michigan from celiac disease, a genetic intestinal disease, on November 16th 2000. He was 26.

The diminutive rapper (he was just 3ft 9in) cited the disorder for his stature. He performed with Kid Rock's backing group, Twisted Brown Trucker. At the Woodstock 1999 performance he sported a t-shirt proclaiming: "I'm Not a Fucking Midgit!"

Despite his ability to handle the disease with black humour, it did require daily medication and treatment.

Roger Durham, singer and drummer with Kansas R&B band Bloodstone, died after falling off a horse in July 27th 1973. He was 27.

Bass player with Aussie New Wave bands Birthday Party and Nick Cave & The Bad Seed, **Tracy Pew** died on July 5th 1986 from drink-related illness. He was 28.

Dennis Danell, guitarist of the California punk band Social Distortion, died on February 29th 2000 at his home at Newport Beach, near Los Angeles, after suffering a stroke. He was 38.

Soul crooner **Keith Barrow** died on October 22nd 1983 from Aids. He was 29.

Bass player with Iggy Pop's Detroit band The Stooges, **Dave Alexander** died from pneumonia on February 10th 1975. He was 27.

Keyboard player with Ohio funksters Switch and later DeBarge, **Bobby DeBarge** was jailed for drug dealing in the 1980s and died from Aids on August 16th 1995. He was 39.

Bassist with Eric Clapton's bands from Derek and the Dominos to his abrupt sacking by telegram in 1979, **Carl Radle** died of a kidney infection brought on by alcohol and drug excesses on May 30th the following year (1980). He was 38.

Walter 'Crash' Morgan, a part-time drummer with Ontario band Big Sugar, died of a brain aneurysm on stage during a concert in Waterloo, Iowa on October 6th 1995. He was 35.

SUICIDE

THE coward's way out. A cry for help. Mental instability. Or simply just throwing in the towel. The reasons for suicide can be complex – one of the above or a combination of all three.

A cry for help or attention or understanding is the most common cause, judging by the number of unsuccessful attempts: one American committed suicide for every 25 attempts in 2001.

More whites kill themselves than blacks, more men than women - though, strangely, women are more likely by far to contemplate suicide.

"There is only one prospect worse than being chained to an intolerable existence: The nightmare of a botched attempt to end it" – Hungarian-born philosopher Arthur Koestler. A lifelong advocate of euthanasia, Koestler and his third wife, Cynthia, killed themselves in a suicide pact in London in March 1983. Was Michael Hutchence's existence so intolerable that he felt compelled to end it?

Michael Hutchence, lead singer of INXS, hanged himself in his Sydney hotel room on November 22nd 1997. He was 37.

The previous day he had seemed relaxed and happy as he rehearsed for the band's 20th anniversary tour before having dinner with his father.

New South Wales Coroner Derek Hand reported: "The deceased was found at 11.50am naked behind the door to his room. He had apparently hanged himself with his own belt and the buckle broke away and his body was found kneeling on the floor and facing the door."

A hotel maid had found the body. Earlier that morning, Hutchence had spoken with his girlfriend Paula Yates who was in London awaiting a custody case involving her children and her ex-husband Bob Geldof.

Hutchence told her he was going to beg Geldof to let the children come out to Australia. Yates said he sounded "desperate" during the conversation. He then phoned Geldof, who told the coroner that Hutchence was "hectoring and abusive and threatening" but did not sound depressed. Hutchence was, however, on Prozac to treat his depressions. He had been drinking into the early hours and cocaine was found in his blood.

Badfinger composers **Pete Ham** and **Tom Evans**, who wrote the 1972 Harry Nilsson hit Without You, both committed suicide.

Swansea-born Ham suffered from depression and hanged himself on April 24th 1975 in his garage studio at Weybridge, Surrey. He was 27.

Badfinger disbanded after Ham's death but reformed four years later. They never enjoyed the financial rewards many thought they deserved and Evans hanged himself on November 18th 1983. He was 36.

The band shot to fame in Liverpool – Paul McCartney signed them to Apple Records and helped produce their debut album. The band made several recordings with the individual Beatles and were invited by George Harrison to play at his star-spangled Bangladesh charity bash in New York in 1971.

Biggie Tembo, former vocalist/guitarist with Zimbabwean band Bhundu Boys, hanged himself on August 13th 1995. He was 37.

Tembo had been having treatment for mental illness.

The Bhundus (named after Zimbabwean rebel fighters) received critical acclaim in Britain in the 1980s, but the boys suffered heartbreak with three members succumbing to Aids: bass player David Mankaba, his replacement Shepherd Munyama and drummer Shakespeare Kangwena.

Lush drummer **Chris Acland** hanged himself at his parents' home in Cumbria on October 17th 1996. He was 30.

His body was discovered by his father. An article printed in The Guardian a year after his death claimed Lush band members had been paid a basic wage of just $250 a week, despite their success.

Jon Lee, drummer with British band Feeder, hanged himself in his Miami home on January 7th 2002. He was 33.

Lee had a strained relationship with his wife, Tatiana, and had phoned her to warn: I'm going to do something stupid.

She returned home to find him hanging by a metal dog chain from the rafters of his garage. He had three notes tacked to his shirt.

New York folk singer **Phil Ochs** hanged himself on April 9th 1976. He was 35. Many thought he was talented enough to surpass his contemporary Bob Dylan. However, he could never match Dylan's incredible output and variety, and succumbed to depression.

Rozz Williams, singer with Christian Death, hanged himself in his Hollywood appartment on April 1st 1998. He was 34.

Williams, born Roger Alan Painter, was labelled the king of gothic rock in the 80s. He suffered drink and drugs addiction but friends were surprised by his suicide. His last live performance was a memorial concert in LA in January 1998 for a close friend who had committed suicide the previous year.

James Lawrence, guitarist with British rock band Hope of the States, hanged himself in Bath, Wiltshire on January 15th 2004. He was 26.

His body was found at the Real World Studios – owned by Peter Gabriel – where the band were recording their debut album.

Ian Curtis, singer with British New Wave band Joy Division, hanged himself in the kitchen of his home in Macclesfield on May 18th 1980. He was 23. The band were due to fly to the USA in two days for a tour.

Curtis suffered from depression and epileptic fits – sometimes on stage. He left a note which read: "I wish I were dead. I just can't cope anymore."

His widow, Deborah, wrote a biography Touching From A Distance about Curtis's troubled life and how he ill-treated her.

The three remaining members changed their name to New Order the following year and continued recording and touring.

Singer/composer **Billy Nelson**, son of country great Willie, hanged himself in Nashville on Christmas Day 1991. He was 33. The previous year he had received hospital treatment for chronic alcoholism.

Paul Williams, singer with Motown legends The Temptations, shot himself in his car in Detroit on August 17th 1973. He was 34.

Williams, who hailed from Birmingham, Alabama had a battle against the bottle and also suffered from Sickle Cell Anaemia – a serious blood disorder which affected him when flying and forced him to quit touring.

Ronald Koal, flamboyant frontman with Ohio band The Trillionaires, shot himself on May 8th 1993. He was 33.

Frank Zappa once told Koal: "You make David Bowie look like a faker."

John Spence, founder and singer with Californian reggae band No Doubt, shot himself in a car park in Anaheim on December 21st 1987. He was 18. 'No Doubt' took their name after a phrase Spence used frequently. The band were set for their first headline show when he killed himself.

Producer **Joe Meek**, hailed as the British Phil Spector, killed his landlady and then himself on February 3rd 1967. He was 37.

Meek was taking medication for mental problems when he shot Violet Shenton, 54, at her home on Holloway Road, London. The inquest heard that 24 bottles of pills were found in his room.

Why he killed Mrs Shenton is unclear. She had gone up to his room to see him and had been there several minutes before one of Meek's assistants, Patrick Pink, heard a shot and then saw Mrs Shenton fall down the stairs.

A second shot rang out as Meek turned the shotgun on himself. Meek died instantly; Mrs Shenton en route to hospital. Meek was obsessed by Buddy Holly who had died in a plane crash eight years previously to the day. He claimed to have been in contact with Holly via séances. Meek's biggest claims to fame were Telstar (Tornados) which became the first USA number one by a British group, and Have I The Right? (Honeycombs).

Chuck Wagon (born Bob Davis), keyboard player with Californian punk band The Dickies, shot himself in December 1981. He was 24.

Doug Hopkins, founder of Arizona band Gin Blossoms, shot himself with a .38 pistol in his Tempe appartment on December 4th 1993. He was 32.

Hopkins had been fired from the band the previous April because of his drinking problems. Shortly afterwards his last single with the band, Hey Jealousy, went gold. Hopkins destroyed the gold plaque.

The day before his death he had left a rehab clinic and bought the pistol from a pawn. shop. His body was found the following morning by friend Lawrence Zubia, who had worked with Hopkins in The Chimeras.

"Me and Doug made a deal in the last eight days that he would not lock his front door, because he was now living alone," Zubia said, adding that Hopkins's girlfriend had moved out.

"That's why I became very concerned at this point. I put my life on hold for the past week. He had lost everything through drinking."

Hopkins's sister, Sara, said this was his sixth suicide attempt in 10 years. She had gone to his appartment on December 2nd and found the Yellow Pages open at gun-shop adverts.

Jason Thirsk, bass player with Californian punk band Pennywise, shot himself after a drinking session on July 29th, 1996. He was 27. His girlfriend discovered the body in the backyard of his home at Hermosa Beach, California. Thirsk had been depressed since leaving the band that year.

Sims Ellison, bass player with Texas rock band Pariah, shot himself on June 5th 1995. He was 28. Sims formed Pariah with his younger brother Kyle. He suffered from depression which increased as the band's record label refused to provide the promised backing.

He shot himself in the head shortly after Pariah had played their final gig.

Nickolas Traina, vocalist with Californian punk band Link 80, killed himself with a drug overdose on September 21st 1997. He was 19.

Traina, son of writer Danielle Steel, had been receiving treatment for mental illness and drug addiction for five years from therapist Julie Campbell.

Traina lived in a cottage behind Campbell's Berkeley home. It was Campbell's husband who discovered the body.

A syringe was found next to his body, and a spoon with a burned residue and a cotton ball were lying nearby, authorities said. All are consistent with heroin use. Danielle Steel told a local paper: "The only time he messed around with drugs was when his medications failed him and he was desperate. This was not some wild kid, this was a very sick kid.

"The awful thing is I knew for years. He was manic-depressive. He wrestled with mental illness all his life."

Campbell said: "In the last five years, my job has been Nick. Three years ago, he moved in. When he was well enough to stay on his own, he stayed in the cottage, but most nights he stayed in the house. Two full-time psychiatric attendants were there to help, too."

Lead singer with Scottish band The Associates, **Billy MacKenzie** killed himself with a drug overdose at his parents' home on January 23rd 1997. He was 39. One of the most highly-rated singers to come out of Scotland, MacKenzie was an eccentric bisexual – his passions included breeding dogs and collecting cars, even though he didn't drive.

Robert Pilatus, one half of the controversial German duo Milli Vanilli, killed himself with an overdose of drink and drugs in a Frankfurt hotel room on April 2nd 1998. He was 32.

Milli Vanilli were stripped of their 1989 Grammy award (for best new artist) when it was revealed that they had not actually sung on their recordings. Pilatus, son of an American soldier and a German stripper, had tried suicide previously and been ordered to undergo drug rehab after being convicted of sexually assaulting a 25-year-old woman in Los Angeles.

"Musically, we are more talented than any Bob Dylan," Pilatus told Time magazine in 1990. "Musically, we are more talented than Paul McCartney. Mick Jagger, his lines are not clear. He don't know how he should produce a sound. I'm the new modern rock 'n' roll. I'm the new Elvis."

Merseyside band leader **Rory Storm** killed himself on September 27th 1973. He was 32. His mother was also found dead in the home, sparking stories of a suicide pact.

Rory Storm & The Hurricanes – Ringo Starr was their drummer before joining The Beatles – were in at the start of the Liverpool scene but never enjoyed the success many feel they warranted and split in 1967.

Rory became a disc jockey, travelling to European clubs and holiday resorts. He was working in Amsterdam when he received the news that his father had died. He returned home to be with his mother, Violet.

He is believed to have taken some sleeping pills and died in his sleep. His mother found him dead and took an overdose.

Guitarist **William Tucker** committed suicide by taking pills and heroin and then slitting his own throat in his Chicago apartment on May 14th 1999. He was 38. Tucker, born in New Jersey and known for his work with

Ministry and Pigface among others, had been suffering from a mystery ailment. A roommate discovered a ten-page suicide note by his body.

British singer/song-writer **Nick Drake** died from a overdose of anti-depressants in his parents' home in Tanworth-in-Arden, near Birmingham, on November 25th 1974. He was 26.

The coroner's suicide verdict surprised many.

Nick's sister, Gabrielle, featured in many TV series, including The Avengers and The Brothers.

Liverpool crooner **Michael Holliday**, who had several hits, including Stairway of Love, committed suicide on 29th October 1963 by taking a drug overdose in Croydon, Surrey. He was 34.

British soul singer **Ephraim Lewis** killed himself on March 18th, 1994 by jumping from the balcony of a Los Angeles apartment. He was 26.

Due to the mysterious circumstances of his death, it would be a month before his burial could take place in his home-town of Wolverhampton. Lewis's family blamed the LAPD, Elektra Records and his manager David Harper for his death.

Lewis – hailed as the British Michael Jackson – was in a happy mood when he left for LA in 1994 to work on new material. He had left his girlfriend, come out of the closet and moved in with a boyfriend.

He enjoyed the gay scene in California but there has been no confirmed explanation for his bizarre behaviour on the day of his death. Cops were called to a Hollywood appartment building on Fuller Avenue where a naked man was acting crazy. It was 7am and Lewis, who was due to fly back to the UK that day, was singing and jumping from balcony to balcony.

He shouted abuse at police when they arrived. After an hour, police fired a taser (stun gun) which hit Lewis. But they insist that was not responsible for his jump/fall to the courtyard. Medics tried to save him in vain and he was pronounced dead shortly before midnight.

David Savoy, manager of American punk band Husker Du, killed himself by jumping off a bridge in Minneapolis in February 1987. He was 24.

The band had struggled to come to terms with drink and drug problems combined with internal rivalries but were scheduled to start a US tour when Savoy died.

American soul singer **Donny Hathaway** committed suicide on January 13th 1979. He was 33. The glass had been carefully removed from his window before he jumped from the 15th floor of New York's Essex House hotel. Hathaway had solo success and also recorded chart hits like Where Is The Love? with Roberta Flack – a contemporary of his at university in Washington. Hathaway had treatment for mental problems.

The year after his death a duet with Flack - Back Together Again - reached number Three in the UK charts.

Don Drummond, trombonist with reggae band The Skatalites, committed suicide in a mental hospital on May 6th 1969. He was 26. He had been committed to Kingston's Bellevue Hospital after murdering his girlfriend, 23-year-old Anita Mahfood (an exotic dancer aka Margarita), five years before.

There was outrage at his memorial service when a friend, Supersonics drummer Hugh Malcolm, tore up the death certificate. Malcolm was among many who believed Drummond had been murdered by guards.

Drummond had told police Margarita had killed herself (he actually went to the police station to report the death). Officers returned home with Drummond to find Margarita lying on the bed and with a knife still stuck in her chest and her hand thrust inside Drummond's trombone.

Drummond was declared insane at his trial.

Singer-songwriter **Elliott Smith** killed himself with a single stab wound to the chest on October 21st 2003. He was 34.

His body was discovered at his Los Angeles home by his girlfriend.

At the time of his death, Smith was recording his sixth album, From A Basement On The Hill.

British jazz/bluesman **Graham Bond** committed suicide on May 8th 1974 by throwing himself into the path of a London Underground train. He was 36. Bond was a troubled man - hooked on drink, drugs and the occult (he formed a band called Holy Magick).

He had worked with some legends of the 1960s British scene: Alexis Korner's Blues Incorporated and Cream's Jack Bruce and Ginger Baker.

Helmut Koellen, bass player with Cologne rock band Triumvirat, died on May 3rd 1977 from carbon monoxide poisoning. He was 27. He died in his garage while listening to tapes from a recording session earlier that day.

Janet Vogel, singer with 1950s Pittsburgh-based The Skyliners, died in her car from carbon monoxide poisoning on February 21st 1980. She was 38.

Jeff Ward, drummer with the aptly-named Chicago band Low Pop Suicide, killed himself on March 19th 1993. He was 30. He had become addicted to heroin and committed suicide by carbon-monoxide poisoning.

Chicago-born **Jim Ellison**, singer and guitar player with Material Issue, killed himself with carbon monoxide fumes from his moped on June 20th 1996. He was 31.

Thomas Wayne Perkins killed himself in car crash near Memphis on August 15th 1971. He was 31. Perkins, who had a hit with Tragedy – recorded by Elvis Presley's guitarist Scotty Moore – deliberately drove his car across four lanes of traffic before crashing into an oncoming vehicle.

John Hunter, drummer with Memphis rock 'n roll band The Hombres, shot himself in February 1976. He was 34.

Let It Out (Let It All Hang Out) reached number 12 in the American charts.

Matthew Fletcher, drummer with British band Heavenly, killed himself at his Oxford home on June 14th 1996. He was 25.

Rick Garberson, drummer with Ohio-based band The Bizarros, poisoned himself on July 15th 1979. He was 28.

Yogi Horton, drummer with Luther Vandross and others, committed suicide on June 8th 1987. He was 33.

Tommy Keiser, bass player with Swiss band Krokus, committed suicide on Christmas Eve 1986. He was 29.

Editor Steve Butterworth is a freelance journalist living in Essex, United Kingdom

Many thanks to all the gracious people who helped.

Special thanks as always to Karla Mahar

MURDER

SUICIDE

BY DATE

Holliday, Michael	October 1963
Meek, Joe	February 1967
Drummond, Don	May 1969
Perkins, Thomas	August 1971
Williams, Paul	August 1973
Storm, Rory	September 1973
Bond, Graham	May 1974
Drake, Nick	November 1974
Ham, Peter	April 1975
Hunter, John	February 1976
Ochs, Phil	April 1976
Koellen, Helmut	May 1977
Hathaway, Donny	January 1979
Garberson, Rick	July 1979
Vogel, Janet	February 1980
Curtis, Ian	May 1980
Chuck Wagon	December 1981
Koal, Ronald	May 1983
Evans, Tom	November 1983
Keiser, Tommy	December 1986
Savoy, David	February 1987
Horton, Yogi	June 1987
Spence, John	December 1987
Ohlin, Per Yngve	April 1991
Nelson, Billy	December 1991
Ward, Jeff	March 1993
Hopkins, Doug	December 1993
Lewis, Ephraim	March 1994
Ellison, Sims	June 1995
Biggie Tembo	August 1995
Fletcher, Matthew	June 1996
Ellison, Jim	June 1996
Thirsk, Jason	July 1996
Acland, Chris	October 1996
Mackenzie, Billy	January 1997
Traina, Nickolas	September 1997
Hutchence, Michael	November 1997
Williams, Rozz	April 1998
Pilatus, Robert	April 1998
Tucker, William	May 1999
Lee, Jon	January 2002
Smith, Elliott	October 2003
Lawrence, James	January 2004

BY AGE

Spence, John	18
Traina, Nickolas	19
Ohlin, Per Yngve	20
Curtis, Ian	23
Chuck Wagon	24
Savoy, David	24
Fletcher, Matthew	25
Drummond, Don	26
Drake, Nick	26
Lewis, Ephraim	26
Lawrence, James	26
Ham, Peter	27
Koellen, Helmut	27
Thirsk, Jason	27
Garberson, Rick	28
Ellison, Sims	28
Keiser, Tommy	29
Ward, Jeff	30
Acland, Chris	30
Perkins, Thomas	31
Ellison, Jim	31
Storm, Rory	32
Hopkins, Doug	32
Pilatus, Robert	32
Hathaway, Donny	33
Koal, Ronald	33
Horton, Yogi	33
Nelson, Billy	33
Lee, Jon	33
Holliday, Michael	34
Williams, Paul	34
Hunter, John	34
Williams, Rozz	34
Smith, Elliott	34
Ochs, Phil	35
Bond, Graham	36
Evans, Tom	36
Meek, Joe	37
Biggie Tembo	37
Hutchence, Michael	37
Vogel, Janet	38
Tucker, William	38
Mackenzie, Billy	39

ACCIDENT

BY DATE

Brown, Milton	April 1936
Ace, Johnny	December 1954
Brown, Clifford	June 1956
Powell, Richie	June 1956
Holly, Buddy	February 1959
Valens, Richie	February 1959
Big Bopper	February 1959
Belvin, Jesse	February 1960
Cochran, Eddie	April 1960
Cline, Patsy	March 1963
Burnette, Johnny	August 1964
Box, David	October 1964
Farina, Richard	April 1966
Kidd, Johnny	October 1966
Redding, Otis	December 1967
Caldwell, Ronnie	December 1967
Cunningham, Carl	December 1967
Jones, Phalin	December 1967
King, Jimmy	December 1967
Lamble, Martin	May 1969
Shorty Long	June 1969
Jones, Brian	July 1969
Stewart, Billy	January 1970
Grant, Earl	June 1970
Allman, Duane	October 1971
Harvey, Les	May 1972
Oakley, Berry	November 1972
White, Clarence	July 1973
Croce, Jim	September 1973
Dey, Rick	November 1973
Rostill, John	November 1973
Bloom, Bobby	February 1974
Chase, Bill	August 1974
Bennett, Duster	March 1976
Relf, Keith	May 1976
Bolan, Marc	September 1977
Van Zant, Ronnie	October 1977
Gaines, Steven	October 1977
Gaines, Cassie	October 1977
Kath, Terry	January 1978
Francois, Claude	March 1978
Kummel, Les	December 1978
Bell, Chris	December 1978
De Fleur, Zenon	March 1979
Arama, Greg	September 1979
Miller, Jacob	March 1980
Caldwell, Tommy	April 1980
Godchaux, Keith	July 1980
Took, Steve	October 1980
Currie, Steve	April 1981

Chapin, Harry	July 1981
Moreve, Rushton	July 1981
Rhoades, Randy	March 1982
Williams, Lamar	January 1983
Rogers, Stan	June 1983
Wilson, Dennis	December 1983
Dingley, Nicholas	December 1984
Watson, Merle	October 1985
Boon, Dennes	December 1985
Chapin, Andy	December 1985
Intveld, Rick	December 1985
Neal, Bobby	December 1985
Woodward, Patrick	December 1985
Burton, Cliff	September 1986
Dornacker, Jane	October 1986
Martin, Dino	March 1987
DeFreitas, Peter	June 1989
Bators, Stiv	June 1990
Vaughan, Stevie Ray	August 1990
Patterson, Roger	February 1991
Will Sin	May 1991
Kinison, Sam	April 1992
Hackman, Paul	July 1992
Oliva, Criss	October 1993
Silk, Garnett	December 1994
Jensen, Ken	January 1995
Albert, Carl	April 1995
Vigliatura, Jack	September 1995
White, Bill	September 1995
Bender, Tim	September 1995
Collins, Rob	July 1996
Hoke, Eldon	April 1997
Taylor, Tim	May 1997
Buckley, Jeff	May 1997
Comeaux, Amie	December 1997
Kelly, Tim	February 1998
Strait, Lynn	December 1998
Kemistry	April 1999
Suba	November 1999
Wick, Jerry	January 2001
Aaliyah	August 2001
Thornton, Melanie	November 2001
Serrano-Serrano, Maria	November 2001
Van het Ende, Nathaly	November 2001
Butthole, Bianca	December 2001
Waddell, Doreen	March 2002
Lopes, Lisa	April 2002
Hansen, Mary	December 2002
Longley, Ty	February 2003
Raimoranta, Teemu	March 2003
Rip Thrillby	May 2003

ACCIDENT

Valens, Richie	17		Jensen, Ken	29
Cunningham, Carl	18		Cline, Patsy	30
Jones, Phalin	18		Burnette, Johnny	30
King, Jimmy	18		Croce, Jim	30
Caldwell, Ronnie	19		Bolan, Marc	30
Lamble, Martin	19		Caldwell, Tommy	30
Cochran, Eddie	21		Oliva, Criss	30
Box, David	21		Buckley, Jeff	30
Vigliatura, Jack	21		Strait, Lynn	30
Comeaux, Amie	21		Lopes, Lisa	30
Holly, Buddy	22		Rostill, John	31
Intveld, Rick	22		Kath, Terry	31
Patterson, Roger	22		Took, Steve	31
Aaliyah	22		Will Sin	31
White, Bill	23		Brown, Milton	32
Bender, Tim	23		Godchaux, Keith	32
Big Bopper	24		Longley, Ty	32
Allman, Duane	24		Chapin, Andy	33
Oakley, Berry	24		Stewart, Billy	33
Dingley, Nicholas	24		Relf, Keith	33
Burton, Cliff	24		Kummel, Les	33
Ace, Johnny	25		Moreve, Rushton	33
Powell, Richie	25		Rogers, Stan	33
Dey, Rick	25		Albert, Carl	33
Raimoranta, Teemu	25		Collins, Rob	33
Brown, Clifford	26		Wick, Jerry	33
Redding, Otis	26		Currie, Steve	34
Miller, Jacob	26		Williams, Lamar	34
Rhoades, Randy	26		Kelly, Tim	34
Belvin, Jesse	27		Thornton, Melanie	34
Kidd, Johnny	27		Martin, Dino	35
Jones, Brian	27		Vaughan, Stevie Ray	35
Harvey, Les	27		Kemistry	35
Bell, Chris	27		Watson, Merle	36
Boon, Dennes	27		Butthole, Bianca	36
DeFreitas, Peter	27		Waddell, Doreen	36
Serrano-Serrano, Maria	27		Hansen, Mary	36
Van het Ende, Nathaly	27		Rip Thrillby	36
Bloom, Bobby	28		Grant, Earl	37
Gaines, Steven	28		Woodward, Patrick	37
De Fleur, Zenon	28		Chapin, Harry	38
Silk, Garnett	28		Kinison, Sam	38
Taylor, Tim	28		Neal, Bobby	38
Farina, Richard	29		Suba	38
Shorty Long	29		Chase, Bill	39
White, Clarence	29		Francois, Claude	39
Bennett, Duster	29		Wilson, Dennis	39
Van Zant, Ronnie	29		Dornacker, Jane	39
Gaines, Cassie	29		Bators, Stiv	39
Arama, Greg	29		Hackman, Paul	39
			Hoke, Eldon	39

DRUGS

BY DATE

Beiderbecke, Bix	August 1931
Parker, Charlie	March 1955
Washington, Dinah	December 1963
Lewis, Rudy	May 1964
Epstein, Brian	August 1967
Lymon, Frankie	February 1968
Wilson, Al	September 1970
Hendrix, Jimi	September 1970
Joplin, Janis	October 1970
Baby Huey	October 1970
Morrison, Jim	July 1971
Cole, Brian	February 1972
Miss Christine	November 1972
Murcia, Bill	November 1972
Whitten, Danny	November 1972
McKernan, Ron	March 1973
Parsons, Gram	September 1973
Taylor, Vinnie	April 1974
McIntosh, Robbie	September 1974
Buckley, Tim	June 1975
Thain, Gary	December 1975
Kossoff, Paul	March 1976
Bolin, Tommy	December 1976
Herbert, Gregory	January 1978
Moon, Keith	September 1978
Vicious, Sid	February 1979
Scott, Bon	February 1980
Owen, Malcolm	July 1980
Bonham, John	September 1980
Darby Crash	December 1980
Hardin, Tim	December 1980
Bloomfield, Mike	February 1981
Hite, Bob	April 1981
Honeyman-Scott, J	June 1982
Farndon, Peter	April 1983
Givens, Candy	January 1984

Byron, David	February 1985
Holton, Gary	October 1985
Rudetski, Michael	August 1987
Shatter, Will	December 1987
Slovak, Hillel	June 1988
Whitley, Keith	May 1989
Wood, Andrew	March 1990
Graves, Rob	June 1990
Mydland, Brent	July 1990
Clark, Steve	January 1991
Thunders, Johnny	April 1991
Preston, Nigel	May 1992
Ondras, Charlie	June 1992
Sargent, Stefanie	June 1992
Helno	January 1993
Allin, G.G.	June 1993
Jones, Rob	July 1993
Cobain, Kurt	April 1994
Pfaff, Kirsten	June 1994
Montgomery, Ken	September 1994
Kelly, Wells	October 1994
Stinson, Bob	February 1995
Goettel, Dwayne	August 1995
Hoon, Shannon	October 1995
Nowell, Bradley	May 1996
Melvoin, Jonathan	July 1996
Crosby, Dawn	December 1996
Arkeen, West	May 1997
Epic Soundtracks	November 1997
Butler, Lester	May 1998
DJ Screw	November 2000
Crack, Carl	September 2001
Foley, Zac	January 2002
Staley, Layne	April 2002
Montague	May 2003
Ward, Jeremy	May 2003

DRUGS

BY AGE

Darby Crash	21
Murcia, Bill	21
Vicious, Sid	21
Miss Christine	22
McIntosh, Robbie	24
Sargent, Stefanie	24
Wood, Andrew	24
Bolin, Tommy	25
Honeyman-Scott, J	25
Lymon, Frankie	25
Taylor, Vinnie	25
Baby Huey	26
Kossoff, Paul	26
Owen, Malcolm	26
Parsons, Gram	26
Slovak, Hillel	26
Thain, Gary	26
Cobain, Kurt	27
Cole, Brian	27
Hendrix, Jimi	27
Joplin, Janis	27
Lewis, Rudy	27
McKernan, Ron	27
Morrison, Jim	27
Pfaff, Kirsten	27
Rudetski, Michael	27
Ward, Jeremy	27
Wilson, Al	27
Beiderbecke, Bix	28
Buckley, Tim	28
Hoon, Shannon	28
Nowell, Bradley	28
Helno	29
Jones, Rob	29
Whitten, Danny	29
Clark, Steve	30

Crack, Carl	30
DJ Screw	30
Farndon, Peter	30
Graves, Rob	30
Herbert, Gregory	30
Foley, Zac	31
Goettel, Dwayne	31
Montague	31
Shatter, Will	31
Bonham, John	32
Epstein, Brian	32
Moon, Keith	32
Crosby, Dawn	33
Preston, Nigel	33
Scott, Bon	33
Whitley, Keith	33
Melvoin, Jonathan	34
Parker, Charlie	34
Staley, Layne	34
Holton, Gary	35
Kelly, Wells	35
Stinson, Bob	35
Allin, G.G.	36
Arkeen, West	36
Hite, Bob	36
Montgomery, Ken	36
Ondras, Charlie	36
Bloomfield, Mike	37
Mydland, Brent	37
Butler, Lester	38
Byron, David	38
Epic Soundtracks	38
Givens, Candy	38
Thunders, Johnny	38
Hardin, Tim	39
Washington, Dinah	39

MEDICAL

BY DATE

Lang, Eddie	March 1933
Rodgers, Jimmie	May 1933
Webb, Chick	June 1939
Williams, Hank	January 1953
Willis, Chuck	April 1958
Sutcliff, Stu	April 1962
Davies, Cyril	January 1964
Black, Bill	October 1965
Berns, Bert	December 1967
Hale, Malcolm	October 1968
Terrell, Tammi	March 1970
McNair, Harold	March 1971
McPherson, Don	July 1971
Baker, Lefty	August 1971
Vincent, Gene	October 1971
Parker, Junior	November 1971
McPhatter, Clyde	June 1972
Durham, Roger	July 1973
Darin, Bobby	December 1973
Elliott, Cass	July 1974
Alexander, Dave	February 1975
Ballard, Florence	February 1976
Powell, William	May 1977
Laughner, Peter	June 1977
Denny, Sandy	April 1978
Patto, Mike	March 1979
George, Lowell	June 1979
McCoy, Van	July 1979
Riperton, Minnie	July 1979
McCulloch, Jimmy	September 1979
Glascock, John	November 1979
Radle, Carl	May 1980
Goodson, Ronnie	November 1980
Chandler, Kermit	February 1981
Marley, Bob	May 1981
Baah, Reebop Kwaku	January 1982

Carpenter, Karen	February 1983
Jobriath	July 1983
Wood, Chris	July 1983
Nomi, Klaus	August 1983
Barrow, Keith	October 1983
Jans, Tom	March 1984
Goodman, Steve	September 1984
Wilson, Ricky	October 1985
Lynott, Phil	January 1986
Pew, Tracy	July 1986
Lyall, Billy	December 1986
Snakefinger	July 1987
Gibb, Andy	March 1988
Murphy, Alan	October 1989
Appleby, Mel	January 1990
Collins, Allen	January 1990
Sohl, Richard	June 1990
MacLeod, Brian	April 1992
Porcaro, Jeff	August 1992
Waite, Patrick	February 1993
Gillen, Ray	December 1993
McDonnell, Sean	January 1995
DeBarge, Bobby	August 1995
Morgan, Crash	October 1995
Ashman, Matthew	November 1995
Robinson, Darren	December 1995
Pierce, Jeffrey Lee	March 1996
Petola, Ilari	September 1996
Big Pun	February 2000
Danell, Dennis	February 2000
Joe C	November 2000
Schuldiner, Chuck	December 2001
Williams, Dave	August 2002
Hannon, Terome	September 2003
Lofstrom, Mary	October 2003

MEDICAL

Sutcliff, Stu	21
Ganser, Mary-Ann	22
Appleby, Mel	23
Laughner, Peter	24
Terrell, Tammi	24
Waite, Patrick	24
Brian, Ty	26
Joe C	26
McCulloch, Jimmy	26
Alexander, Dave	27
Durham, Roger	27
Big Pun	28
Glascock, John	28
Pew, Tracy	28
Robinson, Darren	28
Baker, Lefty	29
Barrow, Keith	29
Lang, Eddie	29
McDonnell, Sean	29
McPherson, Don	29
Williams, Hank	29
Gibb, Andy	30
Petola, Ilari	30
Webb, Chick	30
Williams, Dave	30
Willis, Chuck	30
Davies, Cyril	31
Denny, Sandy	31
Riperton, Minnie	31
Ballard, Florence	32
Carpenter, Karen	32
Elliott, Cass	32
Rodgers, Jimmie	32
Wilson, Ricky	32
Gillen, Ray	33
Goodson, Ronnie	33

Ferguson, Michael	34
George, Lowell	34
Lynott, Phil	34
Schuldiner, Chuck	34
Ashman, Matthew	35
Jans, Tom	35
Morgan, Crash	35
Murphy, Alan	35
Powell, William	35
Goodman, Steve	36
Lyall, Billy	36
Marley, Bob	36
Patto, Mike	36
Vincent, Gene	36
Chandler, Kermit	37
Collins, Allen	37
Darin, Bobby	37
Hale, Malcolm	37
Jobriath	37
Pierce, Jeffrey Lee	37
Sohl, Richard	37
Baah, Reebop Kwaku	38
Berns, Bert	38
Danell, Dennis	38
Lofstrom, Mary	38
Nomi, Jlaus	38
Porcaro, Jeff	38
Radle, Carl	38
Snakefinger	38
Black, Bill	39
DeBarge, Bobby	39
Hannon, Terome	39
MacLeod, Brian	39
McCoy, Van	39
McNair, Harold	39
McPhatter, Clyde	39
Parker, Junior	39
Wood, Chris	39

INDEX

INDEX

INDEX

NAME	DATE	CAUSE	AGE	PAGE
Hite, Bob	05 April 1981	Drugs	36	44
Hoke, Eldon	19 April 1997	Accident	39	27
Holliday, Michael	29 October 1963	Suicide	34	79
Holly, Buddy	03 February 1959	Accident	22	20
Holton, Gary	25 October 1985	Drugs	35	48
Honeyman-Scott, J	16 June 1982	Drugs	25	46
Hoon, Shannon	21 October 1995	Drugs	28	57
Hopkins, Doug	04 December 1993	Suicide	32	77
Horton, Yogi	08 June 1987	Suicide	33	81
Hunter, John	// February 1976	Suicide	34	81
Hutchence, Michael	22 November 1997	Suicide	37	74
Intveld, Rick	31 December 1985	Accident	22	25
Jackson, Al	01 October 1975	Murder	39	14
Jam Master Jay	30 October 2002	Murder	37	16
Jans, Tom	25 March 1984	Medical	35	65
Jeffreys, Paul	21 December 1988	Murder	36	15
Jensen, Ken	28 January 1995	Accident	29	35
Jobriath	// July 1983	Medical	37	66
Joe C	16 November 2000	Medical	26	72
Johnson, Robert	16 April 1938	Murder	27	7
Jones, Brian	03 July 1969	Accident	27	36
Jones, Phalin	10 December 1967	Accident	18	23
Jones, Rob	30 July 1993	Drugs	29	57
Joplin, Janis	04 October 1970	Drugs	27	43
Kath, Terry	23 January 1978	Accident	31	38
Keiser, Tommy	24 December 1986	Suicide	29	81
Kelly, Tim	05 February 1998	Accident	34	33
Kelly, Wells	29 October 1994	Drugs	35	59
Kemistry	26 April 1999	Accident	35	28
Kidd, Johnny	07 October 1966	Accident	27	31
King Curtis	13 August 1971	Murder	37	13
King, Jimmy	10 December 1967	Accident	18	23
King, Phil	27 April 1972	Murder	27	12
Kinison, Sam	10 April 1992	Accident	38	33
Koal, Ronald	08 May 1983	Suicide	33	76
Koellen, Helmut	03 May 1977	Suicide	27	80
Kossoff, Paul	19 March 1976	Drugs	26	78
Kummel, Les	18 December 1978	Accident	33	34
Lamble, Martin	12 May 1969	Accident	19	30
Lang, Eddie	26 March 1933	Medical	29	72
Laughner, Peter	22 June 1977	Medical	24	72
Lawrence, James	15 January 2004	Suicide	26	76
Lee, Jon	07 January 2002	Suicide	33	75
Lewis, Ephraim	18 March 1994	Suicide	26	79
Lewis, Rudy	20 May 1964	Drugs	27	44
Little Walter	15 February 1968	Murder	37	8
Lofstrom, Mary	20 October 2003	Medical	38	70
Longley, Ty	20 February 2003	Accident	32	35
Lopes, Lisa	26 April 2002	Accident	30	31
Lyall, Billy	// December 1986	Medical	36	66
Lymon, Frankie	27 February 1968	Drugs	25	54
Lynott, Phil	04 January 1986	Medical	34	65
MacKenzie, Billy	23 January 1997	Suicide	39	78
MacLeod, Brian	25 April 1992	Medical	39	68
Marley, Bob	11 May 1981	Medical	36	67
Martin, Dino	21 March 1987	Accident	35	24
McCoy, Van	06 July 1979	Medical	39	66
McCulloch, Jimmy	27 September 1979	Medical	26	63
McDonnell, Sean	18 January 1995	Medical	29	72
McIntosh, Robbie	23 September 1974	Drugs	24	51
McKernan, Ron	08 March 1973	Drugs	27	44
McNair, Harold	26 March 1971	Medical	39	68
McPhatter, Clyde	13 June 1972	Medical	39	63
McPherson, Don	04 July 1971	Medical	29	71
Meek, Joe	03 February 1967	Suicide	37	76
Melvoin, Jonathan	11 July 1996	Drugs	34	45

INDEX

INDEX

Also Published by Eye 5

Brits & Bobs: Bob Dylan In The British Isles

by STEVE BUTTERWORTH

SCATE: Speed Cameras Are The Enemy

by TOM J SANDY